A UNIFIED THEORY OF CATS
ON THE INTERNET

A UNIFIED THEORY OF CATS ON THE INTERNET

E. J. WHITE

stanford briefs
An Imprint of Stanford University Press
Stanford, California

Stanford University Press
Stanford, California

Printed in the United States of America
on acid-free, archival-quality paper

Cataloging-in-Publication Data available on request.

Library of Congress Control Number: 2020937819

ISBN: 9-781-5036-0463-6 (paper)

Cover design: Michel Vrana

Typeset by Classic Typography in 11/15 Adobe Garamond

Well, if you had a very long cat, reaching from New York to Albany, and you trod on its tail in New York, it would throw out a wail in Albany. That's telegraphy; and wireless is precisely the same thing without the cat.

—"Headquarters Notes," *The Commercial Telegraphers' Journal*, ed. Frank B. Powers, vol. 22 (April 1924): 143

CONTENTS

A UNIFIED THEORY OF CATS

ON THE INTERNET

INTRODUCTION

Some time ago, I read through ten years' worth of the *New York Times* best-seller list and noticed a strange phenomenon. Over the previous ten years—from December 17, 2006 to December 17, 2016—fifteen nonfiction books about dogs had been on the *New York Times* best-seller list, altogether spending a total of 118 weeks on the list.[1] During the same period, exactly one best-selling nonfiction book was about a cat. It was on the list for two weeks.[2]

That dogs can anchor best sellers is not surprising. (By now, even those who have not read *Marley and Me* directly have read it by osmosis.) What is surprising is *how many* of them they anchor, especially in light of the undisputed sway that cats hold over the World Wide Web. While dogs have been quietly dominating the world of print, users of the internet have cast their vote— again and again, in the form of millions upon millions of image macros, emojis, memetic videos, and eight-bit Nyan Cats bobbing across the screen—for the cat as the mascot of the digital world. Dogs are from books, cats are from bytes. How has this come to be the case?

The triumph of cats on the internet is a measurable fact; but it is also a myth, a signifier that carries remarkable force in the marketplace of attention. Lolcats, the most famous of internet memes, have become an industry in their own right, producing endless merchandise in the form of T-shirts, posters, mugs, and books—even a Lolcat Bible. Indeed, Lolcats arguably *invented* the popular concept of the internet meme, and for many internet users—especially "digital immigrants," or people who were already in adulthood when they began to use the internet—they constitute the entire experience of internet memes. At the time of this book's writing, most of the celebrity animals on the internet are cats; famous cats online include Maru, Curious Zelda, Hamilton the moustache cat, Venus, Colonel Meow, and the late Lil Bub and Grumpy Cat.[3] Grumpy Cat had merchandise, a movie, and friends in high places: when she passed, the worlds of new media and old media mourned alike.

The invocation of the cat as the mascot of the internet—the internet's "spirit animal," as the *Washington Post* said in 2014—can be used, and often is used, as a free-floating signifier.[4] The poet Kenneth Goldsmith's book *Wasting Time on the Internet* (2016) has an image of a kitten on its cover, though the book doesn't mention cats once.[5] The publisher understood when selecting the cover that the public would understand the symbol without explanation.[6] The *Economist* and the *New York Times* have likewise used images of cats to illustrate articles about the internet that mentioned cats fleetingly, if at all; cats simply provided a shorthand, a symbol for new media that even the newspapers' old-media readerships would be able to understand.[7]

In a 2013 article in *Foreign Policy*, Ben Smith, the editor-in-chief of BuzzFeed News, used a similar shorthand to make a point about the web and the future of journalism: "When I came to BuzzFeed at the end of 2011, some wondered why I would jump from the hard-news hub Politico to a site best known for its appreciation of Ryan Gosling and discerning taste in cat pictures." Here, the phrase *cat pictures* signifies the frivolous side of the internet; the phrase is meant to be a trifle demeaning—a jab, for the benefit of readers who think serious ideas must have serious expression, at the shallowness and pointlessness of much of the content to be found online. New media can accommodate both serious work and pointless leisure, Smith assured his readers: "So don't make the mistake of thinking that just because the social web is full of cat pictures, great journalism is dying."[8]

The advertising slogan of Reddit, a popular social news site, is "Come for the cats. Stay for the empathy."[9] Journalists regularly repeat the joke, "As we all know, the internet is made of cats."[10] BuzzFeed ranks contributors according to a metric that it calls "cat power."[11] (For a time, the metric appeared beside every contributor's byline in the form of a ranking of one to five cats, represented by images of celebrity cats such as Grumpy Cat,

Lil Bub, and Colonel Meow.) The BuzzFeed website explains: "As you know, the internet is powered primarily by cats, so your Cat Power on BuzzFeed is an official measure of your rank in BuzzFeed's Community. The more you are featured and the better you get at making awesome posts, the higher your Cat Power will be."[12]

That BuzzFeed circulates about the same proportions of cat and dog pictures makes no difference to the phrase's significance; indeed, we might measure the cat's power as a symbol of the internet precisely in the *distance* between its usage as a market-facing symbol of the internet—used in cover illustrations; in titles; in journalistic ledes; in knowing throwaway references—and the quantifiable realities that increasingly fail to back up the tacit claims of that usage.

Consider an experiment at Google's bleeding-edge X-Lab in 2012: researchers performed an experiment in "deep learning" to determine whether a computer could learn to recognize shapes and concepts without first being fed training data that had been labeled with those shapes and concepts. Researchers used three concepts to test the computer's neural network: a human face, a human body, and a cat.[13] (The experiment was successful; after looking at 20,000 randomly chosen video thumbnails from YouTube, the neural network generated a Shroud-of-Turin-like digital image of an average cat face for use in recognizing cats. "We never told it during the training, 'This is a cat,'" one researcher told the *New*

York Times. "It basically invented the concept of a cat.")[14] The fact that Google researchers, given a colossally ambitious AI, decided that one of the first things the AI should learn is how to recognize cats says a lot about geek culture and the social norms of the internet age.

Traditional media institutions have taken notice of geek culture's embrace of cats. In 2005, the *New York Times* declared, "Cats are the Web's it-animals. They're everywhere."[15] In 2013, *CBS News* ran a television news story, titled "Cat videos take over the Internet, marketing world," that repeated an unverifiable statistic from the pet food company Friskies: "Fifteen percent of all internet traffic is connected to cats."[16] That same year, an advertising agency announced, in a satirical video, that it was opening a division dedicated to cat videos. "Everything is moving towards cat videos," the video announces. "By 2015, cat videos are going to represent 90% of the content on the World Wide Web. That's proven results."[17]

These trends have prompted serious media scholars to devise theories about the internet that are also theories about cats. The civic media scholar Ethan Zuckerman describes his most widely cited argument about censorship and participatory media as the "cute cat theory of digital activism." (In one of the paper's subheaders, he declares, tongue-in-cheek, "The Internet is Made of Cats.")[18] In 2011, Kate Miltner, a graduate student at the London School of Economics—now a notable media scholar—wrote a master's thesis on Lolcats.[19] In 2015, the

Museum of the Moving Image in New York City held an exhibition, curated by the brilliant Jason Eppink, on "How Cats Took over the Internet."[20]

The rise of what *Wired* magazine has called "the online cat-industrial complex" becomes even more puzzling when viewed against the dog-industrial complex of print media.[21] I regarded this dissimilarity, at first, as evidence that my prejudices against cats—I am a lifelong dog owner—were valid. Why shouldn't books, which are, if not *better* than digital communication, certainly more considered, more thoughtful, demanding of greater commitment, flourish under the Dog Star? Books are machines of *longue durée*, immersing the reader in forms of attention so sustained that they can emulate real experience. In their famous loyalty, dogs likewise give us an experience of sustained attention. But as I fell deeper into the world of cats on the internet and internet cats, I came believe that the question of how cats came to dominate the internet is more profound than it first appears.

A Unified Theory of Cats on the Internet is the first book to explore the history of how the cat came to be the undisputed mascot of the internet. The book has a rough chronological structure, with each chapter exploring specific topics that track with the history of the cat as an instrument of what Dick Hebdige, borrowing from Umberto Eco, termed "semiotic guerilla warfare."[22] The argument that runs through the book's many episodes is that the study of internet cats, as an extension of the study of communities that shaped the world of digital computing, can tell us much about how culture shapes, and is shaped by, technology. Westerners have used cats for centuries as symbols of pathos, anger, and alienation. The communities that helped to build the internet, whose members construed themselves as outsiders who worked against the mainstream, made snark and alienation a part of their identity. Because communication drives so much of the internet, from the microlevel of symbol processing to the macrolevel of media platforms, the history of internet cats is entwined with the social and technological history of the internet at large.

For the purposes of this book, perhaps the most significant aspect of that history is what now seems self-evident, yet once seemed counterintuitive: that the internet's functions are social. "One of the surprising properties of computing," the *Harvard Business Review* reported in 1986, "is that it is a social activity." Organizations that gave employees computers had found that people wanted to use the new technologies to chat, tool around, and pursue generalist questions, not specialist answers: "People usually perceive computers as special-purpose tools for calculations and data storage. But where we have studied computers— in companies and educational organizations—people tend to use them as a general-purpose tool to gather and distribute information and to talk with others."[23]

Cats are a symbol of pointless online sociability; so the reason that we *needed* a symbol of pointless online sociability—that its prevalence came as a surprise to all who had "for so long heard about the coldness and impersonality of the computer"—is worth keeping in mind.[24] From the 1970s to the early 1990s, most research on computer-mediated communication focused on the utilitarian question of whether computers enabled groups in the workplace to carry out tasks more easily. To the bafflement of researchers, the answer was often no.[25] One of the very first books on computer-mediated communication, *The Network Nation* (1978), offers an early glimpse, among the serious work sent over bulletin-board systems on corporate intranets, of the practice, nigh ubiquitous today, of being off-task while online: quips and personal chitchat; funny poems on topical subjects; off-topic, circular, unwinnable arguments; outbursts of obscenity; identity experimentation under pseudonyms; and the circulation of amusing pictures, for instance ASCII art of reindeer to celebrate Christmas.[26]

As *The Network Nation* notes, computer messaging, which lacks personal cues such as body language and facial expressions, puts barriers in the way of humor, emotional expression, and social exchange.[27] But users of ARPANET and other early computer networks evidently found joy in these things, and they put considerable free labor into developing spaces and discourses amenable to them. Early on, mailing lists began to appear on ARPANET that focused on science fiction, wine tasting, and other amusements that could hardly be defended as research.[28] The universities that hosted ARPANET's servers tried to suppress these mailing lists and failed. Frivolous sociability, startling to early observers of computing, became a major force driving the development of the internet: not an epiphenomenon, but a root cause. After all, users liked and wanted it; and since computers, as machines that imitate other machines, are changeful and changeable, the history of digital computing has always arisen, above all, "from the histories of the groups of practitioners who saw in it, or in some yet to be envisioned form of it, the potential to realize their agendas and aspirations."[29]

Internet cats, as a symbol of these agendas—belated as a symbol of frivolity, but timely as a symbol of *japoniste* techno-modernity, youth culture rebellion, cyberpunk aggression, and the weirdness and transgression that once seemed to mark internet culture as an authentic space that was separate from the mainstream—reveal how the communities that adopted networking technologies in advance of the general public helped to establish aesthetic values and social codes that endured in internet culture. They also reveal how, as the general public adopted networking technologies, those early communities sought to raise boundaries between themselves and the newcomers who started to threaten, by their numbers, to dominate new media.

The term *unified theory* is tongue-in-cheek. We can no more unify the frivolity, rebellion, weirdness, and transformative work that takes place on the internet than we can capture the sea in a net. If anything, this book spins a unifying thread from its attention to social division. As historians have shown, major trends in computing have often come, not from mainstream institutions, but from subcultures, countercultures, and upstart startups.[30] An account of internet culture that attends to the history of the idea—now outdated—that a meaningful divide separates the internet from the mainstream can help us to better understand distinctive phenomena that have emerged from the internet, like trolling and memes. It can also help us to better understand how a medium for specialized work, which users adapted to become a medium for sociability, could be adapted still further to become our major delivery system for weirdness. This book investigates that history via the semiotics of online felines, seeking, along the way, to reveal hidden narratives of prejudice, in-group socialization, and cross-cultural identification on the web.

Some initial caveats and a confession.

First, the caveats: this is not a book about cats, but rather a book about the internet. The text gives very little space to the offline lives of cats, and a great deal of space to such themes of new media studies as *mediation, participatory culture*, and *hacker aesthetics*. When I began the research for this book, I took a teetering stack of books about cats out of the library of the College of Veterinary Medicine at Cornell University. ("I have a cat," the library circulation clerk told me. "My friends keep telling me to make her internet famous." Then she showed me a picture of the largest cat I have ever seen.) The books were not much help, it turns out, for understanding internet cats. By contrast, reading about Japan, Silicon

Valley countercultures, punk music, and the sociological concept of boundary maintenance helped a great deal.

Nor does this book account for every cat that has ever won fame on the internet. If I have left out your favorite internet cat, I apologize; I hope this book may nevertheless help you to better enjoy the Niko or Remy or Rolf or Tingeling or Zelda who lights up your digital life.

As a historical commitment, this book tends to emphasize the *lagging edge* as well as the *cutting edge* of high-tech culture. Some of the events I chronicle took the shape they did only because the spread of a new technology was gradual, not immediate. Trolling would not have arisen in the forms it did had the internet not reached the general public years, sometimes decades, after it reached more tech-savvy communities. Meme culture would not have arisen in the forms it did—and cats would not have been at its neo-pop center—had hardcore internet users not built underground, members-only subcultures on hacker forums, image boards, and elsewhere. The narrative in this book relies on an approach to the history of technology that attends to the staggering of early and late adopters, since such staggering can have significant cultural effects.

Another theme of this book is that the internet does not merely *chronicle* cultural events. Cultural events can change the internet at political and even technological levels. Google Images came about because Jennifer Lopez wore a revealing dress to the Grammys in 2000, which created a demand for image-based searching that Google couldn't ignore.[31] Lopez's dress was an event in the history of the internet. YouTube started on the path to what it has today—a natural monopoly over user-generated video—in part because, two days after the platform's public launch in December 2005, *Saturday Night Live* released a hip-hop video, "Lazy Sunday," that seemingly everyone wanted to share with their friends. Bootleg copies of "Lazy Sunday" constituted many people's first experience of YouTube; according to one narrative of YouTube's rise, they helped to carry the platform past a tipping point of market penetration early on.[32]

Cats don't have a monopoly over participatory internet culture as YouTube (nearly) does over internet video. Rather, as Ethan Zuckerman suggests, internet cats resemble long-established web protocols—like the network protocol HTTP, which allows computers to exchange messages for the display of web pages. In most everyday usage, HTTP has been replaced by the more secure network protocol HTTPS, but HTTP is still around, forming the foundational structure of the World Wide Web. Although the explicit identification of cats with the internet is, as this book will show, fairly recent—it dates only to around 2005—by now cats may be, as they say, *baked into* the internet's operations. For the *extremely online*, cats have become a basic part of cultural literacy—a signifier, in Miltner's term, of the *internetty*, or the internet understood as a culture unto itself—while for the rest of the internet's users, cats belong to the suite of online rituals that we perform even if we have forgotten their origin. For the rest of the internet's users, cats belong to the suite of online rituals that we perform even if we have forgotten their origins.

Next, the confession: when I started looking into internet cats, I was a self-avowed cat hater. I used to enjoy ribbing cat owners for keeping companions who (it seemed to me) didn't hold up their end of the bargain. It was an easy posture to take on social media, offering the pleasure of expressing a strong opinion without the risk of expressing an opinion on an important subject. And I had a lot of evidence to work with. Do you see cats carrying little barrels of brandy up mountains to aid lost travelers? Do you see cats herding sheep, protecting cattle, leading the blind, aiding search-and-rescue teams, sniffing out bombs, carrying messages, chasing down suspects, warning off intruders, collecting balls at tennis matches, comforting sick children in the hospital, or pulling drowning sailors from the waves to the shore? No, you don't. My image of dogs corresponded with the works of the painter Edwin Landseer, where dogs are heroes, friends, and mourners; my image of cats corresponded with the works of Salvador Dali, where cats are the useless clocks melting over the furniture.

But then, while researching this book, I took in a cat to foster. A year later, I have to report: I'll grab it, I'll buy it, I'm finally sold. I finally understand what cat people have always been talking about.

Well, I was always a late adopter.

1 THE SEMIOTIC HISTORY OF GRUMPY CATS

One of the notable internet trends of 2015 entailed people making videos of cats being scared by cucumbers. It turns out that cats instinctively fear snakes, which cucumbers resemble—so if you surreptitiously put a cucumber near a cat and wait for the cat to notice, you'll be treated to a nice little freak-out.

The trick is cruel, of course; as animal experts warned, it stresses the cat out.[1] So does *cat breading*, an internet trend that started in 2011 that entails poking a cat's face through a piece of bread and taking a photograph of the result.[2] The spectacle of feline suffering, be it fright or anger, as a form of entertainment is a long tradition, and it shows no sign of fading in the digital age. The tragic cats of the Twitter account "Black Metal Cats," where images with captions make cats seem to ponder grim, depressing thoughts, can seem like a postmodern update on the old convention in Western painting by which cats signified the Devil, witches, the uncanny, the predatory nature of evil (and by which therefore a cat's distress, the panic of a black cat fleeing from the Annunciation, is cause for joy).[3]

Of course, despair is not all we deal out to cats online. Lolcats—a genre of image macros that popularized the concept of the internet meme—often show cats presiding happily over boxes, bubbles, and cheeseburgers. Nyan Cat, an animated character that has become something of a mascot for internet culture, packs the accessories of goofy fun into a single package: he's a cat with a pop tart for a body who flies to a loop of whimsical music, shedding a rainbow contrail. Still, internet cats tend to channel a dark emotional spectrum, even when we use them to represent ourselves. Grumpy Cat gives a face to our snarky comments; Black Metal Cats brood without end, like a teenager listening to a playlist of sad songs on repeat; Lolcats get annoyed, long to be alone, suffer from lack of sleep, and have bad hair days, just like us. Cats can't win: when they're alien to us, they suffer to fuel malicious joy, and when they're projections of us, they suffer to be relatable.

How, by comparison, do we treat dogs on the web? A comparable genre of video—never at the white-hot core of internet fame, but a reliable slow boiler—is the scene of a wagging dog welcoming a soldier home. Or a dog jumping out of a gift box at Christmas, or a dog leaving the pound for a "forever home," or a dog participating, clueless but elated as ever, in a marriage proposal—always happy dogs, always partners in the events of human life.

By common consent, people on the internet find the suffering of dogs not funny, but deeply upsetting. I used to visit an internet forum dedicated to the television series "Game of Thrones"; it was not unusual to see people comment that the deaths of direwolves are the most painful moments of the show to watch. You can find a movie website—titled Does the Dog Die?—whose entire purpose, when it started, was to give visitors a single piece of information about any film: whether a dog in the film dies. No equivalent website exists for cats; indeed, popular cinema has made a trope of killing and injuring cats for comic effect.[4]

In his famous essay "The Great Cat Massacre," Robert Darnton details the long history of making cats suffer as a form of entertainment: we have tossed them into bonfires, hanged them as effigies, held mock trials before putting them to death, and yanked their tails to make "rough music."[5] Darnton conducts a careful semiotic analysis of a strange event in 18th-century Paris, an event, he argues, that can only make sense to moderns if we examine it through semitransparent layers of meaning: a ritual massacre of cats by the apprentices working in a print shop. Darnton traces the symbolic connections that gave this spectacle meaning for the participants: the cats signified, all at once though with the looseness of symbol, witchcraft, the Devil, sexual taboo, the master's household, and the master's wife. The savage ritual "was meant simultaneously as a trial, a gang rape, a rebellion of the workers against their boss, and a carnivalesque kind of street theater, which the workers later repeated in the form of pantomime."[6]

The semiotic connection between cats and evil spirits goes back to the Middle Ages.[7] The same goes for the connection between cats and women's sexuality. The pun that associates cats with women's genitals dates to at least the 15th century and spans several languages, Darnton writes: "*Le chat, la chatte, le minet* mean the same thing in French slang as 'pussy' does in English, and they have served as obscenities for centuries."[8] The cover of Darnton's book displays a painting by François Boucher, "La Toilette" (1742), in which a woman extends her leg to put on a garter. Below, a cat playfully sprawls between her legs—a not-so-subtle symbol that the woman is sexually available.[9] (This punning motif—a cat for a woman's sex—also appears in English pictures: William Hogarth's series "A Harlot's Progress," for example.)

So strong were these iconographic traditions that the appearance of either a cat or a dog in the same painting could point its meaning in opposite directions. The nude woman in Titian's painting *Venus of Urbino* (1534) need not fear our disrespect: a dog sleeping at the woman's feet symbolically assures us that her desire is wedded to fidelity, guarding her against the possibility that her favors might be fickle or for sale.[10] Yet Édouard Manet's painting *Olympia* (1863)—which replicates Titian, with a similar nude reclining in a similar composition—scandalized its first reviewers at the Paris Salon of 1865, who seemed not to notice its connection to Titian but commented, again and again, on the cat that Manet painted at the woman's heels. In fact, the cat dominated the reception of the painting, which thus seemed to be an image of female promiscuity, as the art historian John Moffitt writes: "Owing to an inflammatory combination—leveled female Olympian gaze coupled with an aroused black cat—the general public took all the painter's imagery collectively to explain (according to a much later popular song) 'that's why the lady is a tramp.'" The public often referred to the painting as *Venus au chat noir*.[11] Or again, if viewers saw a dog in a painting of Christ, they had no doubt that the dog was *aligned with* Christ: an emblem of his constancy, warmth, and wit.[12] By contrast, a cat in a painting of Christ signified the Devil as surely as a serpent would.

Folklore extended the idea of cats as agents of trouble. In European folklore, cats have often featured in tale types that warn that the world is full of danger and trickery. For example, in "Death of an elf (or cat)"—tale type 113A in the Aarne-Thompson Uther Tale Type Index, a classification index of Indo-European folktales—a man is walking home one day when he hears an instruction: "When you get home, tell them Grimalkin is dead." The man recognizes neither the voice nor the name, but when he gets home, he complies with the order and announces that Grimalkin is dead. Upon hearing his words, his household cat leaps up and shouts, "Then I am king of the cats!" The cat then vanishes up the chimney, never to be seen again by his former owners.[13]

This tale type includes variations in which a troll or elf serves in place of the cat. As one folklorist argues, cats, trolls, and elves are interchangeable agents for the story's purpose. The lesson of the story is that we must keep watch for malevolent spirits nearby; the man who delivers the message does not expect that his cat will start talking or that trolls live in his home.[14] Even in tales where cats *help* humans, the cat often succeeds through trickery and cunning. In tale type 545 ("the cat as helper"), which we now call "Puss in Boots," a girl or boy who inherits only a cat ends up, through the cat's contrivances, the owner of a castle and the betrothed of a prince or princess. Here, the cat behaves as no animal could: he moves easily in the human social world—indeed, asks for human clothing as his only request—and through social intrigue acquires for his master a genteel, class-conscious happy ending.[15] Like the King of Cats, he is a malevolent spirit hidden in the home; but in this instance, he is a malevolent spirit working *for* us, not against us.[16]

In short, Westerners have long found cats "good to think with," in Claude Levi-Strauss's phrase, and especially to think about the boundary between the mundane world and the world of spirits. The systems that people cultivated for negotiating the dangerous cultural boundaries which cats helped to define ran from folklore to mass entertainment to the ordinary precautions that one might take while caring for a household cat. In the 17th century, an animal expert warned that "the familiars of Witches do most ordinarily appear in the shape of Cats, which is an argument that this beast is dangerous to soul and body." Since cats were of practical use for hunting mice, he advised that "with a wary and discreet eye we must avoid their harms, making more account of their use than of their persons": that is, put them to work, but keep an emotional distance. These were soteriological precautions: precautions concerning the safety of one's soul.[17]

We no longer massacre cats for entertainment, but even today, the torment of cats in fiction is acceptable sport, as one critic observes of tropes in Hollywood films: "When a dog dies, it's a touching and deeply personal moment for the character. We feel their pain. When a cat dies, it's a hilarious joke played for laughs."[18] It's not hard to see the tragic cats of Black Metal Cats, for example, as a postmodern, no-cats-were-harmed-in-the-making-of-this-tweet update on an old tradition. When in 2016 the word *pussy* became unexpectedly a political keyword, the media quickly capitalized on the double meaning of the word: the *New York Daily News* printed the word in enormous letters on its front page, obscuring the middle letters with the seemingly astonished faces of cats.[19] The visual pun was a recognition that the word's connotation of sexuality, its coloring of obscenity, and the low esteem in which popular culture has held the pussy, so to speak, are tied together.

TITS OR GTFO

One of the first recorded instances of mass trolling on the internet was an attack on a forum for cat lovers whose regulars were mostly women. That the women of the cat lovers' forum could seem like outsiders to be pushed from the internet was the outcome of a complex series of gender reversals in the history of computing.

The shift to digital computing changed the gender dynamics of computing as a field; it also had far-reaching effects on the culture of the internet. In the early 20th century, many computers were women; the term *computer* was a job title, referring to someone who worked as a human calculator.[20] Vannevar Bush, in his seminal text "As We May Think" (1945), envisioned the digital computers of the future as large, powerful machines at which human computers ("girls") would perform data entry: "Such machines will have enormous appetites. One of them will take instructions and data from a whole roomful of girls armed with simple key board punches, and will deliver sheets of computed results every few minutes."[21] One of his colleagues suggested, waggishly, that we measure computing power in *kilogirls*, with one kilogirl representing a thousand hours of human work.[22]

During the period of ARPANET's creation and growth in the late 1960s and early 1970s, most of the users of digital computers were professors or military employees, which also meant that they were male. In the early years of the internet's availability to the general public, users made much of its image as a male space. "There are no girls on the internet," ran a common maxim online. If a user revealed herself to be female, she could expect a barrage of messages demanding that she post topless pictures: "Tits or GTFO."

Yet the culture of internet insiders was itself a culture of the alienated, marginalized, and rebellious. By the late 1970s, legislators had enough awareness of computer networking to assign public networks to FCC authority, but, as *The Network Nation* noted, they doubted that networks would attract the interest of lay citizens: "[T]he conception of 'public' currently used by most regulators and legislators is business and government use, and it is not yet conceived that the 'general public' or ordinary citizens will be a market for such systems and that regulations or laws in the public interest should facilitate this."[23] Still, ordinary citizens like the members of the Homebrew Computer Club, which began meeting in a car garage in 1975, were already building a grassroots community of hobbyists who tinkered with home computers and piggybacked on phone lines to connect to networks like Usenet and the Whole Earth 'Lectronic Link (WELL). These tinkerers identified as part of the counterculture, promoting a hacker ethos—a belief that freely exploring information systems would make the world a better place—that ultimately derived from the congenial, obsessive student culture at MIT.[24]

The lay citizens who ran IRC servers, Multi-User Dungeons, and forums on Usenet and the WELL of necessity donated their own funds, equipment, and labor to the cause. This meant they were, largely, hobbyists—and often enthusiasts with passions that the ordinary world couldn't satisfy, but the networked world could. For a time, the "single largest source of income" for the WELL was a conference for fans of the Grateful Dead, who invested substantial capital and technological expertise so they could chat with fellow niche enthusiasts.[25] Deadheads helped to underwrite the early internet.[26]

Over the decades that followed, the identity repertoire of computer geeks embraced many transformations: hacker, science fiction nerd, fantasy nerd, hippie, Deadhead, X-phile, gamer, otaku, Apple fanboy, fanfic writer, techno-libertarian. Yet a consistent theme was a sense of alienation from the mainstream. Then as now, the repertoire of high tech mingled with repertoires from American nerd culture. At MIT, hackers worked on model railroads and built a science-fiction computer game called Spacewar!; when some of them split off to the Stanford AI Lab, they created a lab culture based on high fantasy (influenced perhaps by the crunchy, woodsy ambience of the West Coast): they built a fantasy computer game, named their conference rooms after sites in Middle Earth, and programmed the lab printer to print in Elven lettering.[27] One point of these practices was to be *other*, and at that, proudly, defiantly other; and if that was the message, then a range of idioms could serve equally well for its delivery, from fantasy to punk to the psychedelic counterculture.[28]

INTERNET INSIDERS

Internet denizens choosing an abject, alienated, *catty* animal as their symbol is no more a paradox than punk rockers giving themselves a name that referred—as *punk* did—originally to prostitutes and later to men in the military who did low, contemptuous scut work.[29] Cats can be a symbol of the repulsive, in part because of their association with women. But the countercultural, antiestablishment ethos of the grassroots internet resonated with symbols that aimed to repel.

Nowhere was that ethos more evident than in underground hacker communities, whose members—then as now—portrayed themselves, and were portrayed, as the white-hot center of high tech. A 1990 study of the "computer underground"—that is, bulletin boards devoted to hacking, phreaking, and other "deviant" cyberactivities—observed a spectrum of symbols and practices meant to communicate alienation and revolt.[30] User handles on these boards tended to fall into consistent categories: names that suggested fantasy heroes (Dragon Lord, Ultimate Warrior, Unknown Warrior); names that suggested nihilist antiheroes (Black Avenger, Death Stalker, Storm Bringer); names that incorporated the colors black and red, presumably for their vibe of masculinity and danger; or names that played on references to fantasy, popular culture, or tech (Ellis Dea, Hitch Hacker, Phelix the Hack, Rambo Pacifist). When users formed collectives, they often chose group names with a similar vibe: The Legion of Doom, The Masters of Deception. They gave their bulletin-board systems names like Dragonfire, Forbidden Zone, PHBI, Phreakenstein's Lair, Shadowland, Sherwood Forest, and The Vault.[31] Such names were deliberate provocations, chosen, in Levi-Strauss's term, as "things to whiten mother's hair with."[32]

Scholars who wrote about the computer underground in the 1990s often described it as "postmodern."[33] However, we might more accurately describe it as *punk*.[34] Like postmodern style, the style of the punk subculture was disrespectful, self-reflective, self-aware, ironic, constantly at play, keeping meaning in motion by mixing elements from unlike categories. (In hacker culture, these categories included, for instance, magic and technology, outcast and hero, and apocalypse and victory.) Punk's famous "do it yourself" ethos, which encouraged activities like crafting, clothes-making, music-making under independent labels, and even squatting and shoplifting in order to achieve creative and economic separation from mainstream institutions, cohered with the hands-on, self-reliant ethos of hacker culture.[35] The high schoolers staying up late on underground bulletin boards may not have had ready familiarity with poststructural theory, but the music subculture that had come of age in the 1970s and 1980s was available to every kid with a record player. And punk, despite its surface despair, was forward-looking. From a punk perspective, the past was dishonest, the present was desolate, but the future had possibilities. The future was science fiction.[36]

"The hacker ethic," as Steven Levy terms it, is morally neutral, or even good insofar as it takes care to leaven freedom with responsibility. Its tenets stress self-sufficiency and mistrust of institutions: skills matter, not credentials;

authority is bad and decentralization is good; computers want to be accessible by anyone; information wants to be free; computers are instruments of art; computers can improve the world.[37] Yet the public tended to view the ethos of hackers as careless anarchy, as hackers well knew. The inhabitants of hacker boards celebrated antiheroes because some of them were engaging in criminal activities (e.g., pirating), but also because they were frustrated that the media portrayed hackers almost exclusively as criminals.[38] Nonconformity can be a matter of principle, or an effort to *épater la bourgeoisie*, or a defiant exaggeration of the perception that one is a misfit. Or it can be all three.

This subculture no more defined the boundaries of the wired counterculture than did the hippies of the Homebrew Computer Club, but it provided the counterculture's sharpest edge and its most thrilling characters. Not for nothing was cyberpunk the new dominant genre for stories about the future: Rick Dekkard trudging through a dirty neon city; Henry Case building his own tech to wage asymmetrical warfare against corrupt institutions; Neo Anderson in military boots and black leather; the Lone Gunmen falling into the company of a female hacker with an anarchistic ideology and dramatic fuck-you punk makeup.[39]

Perhaps the online world would have come to absorb, in any version of history, the hostile behaviors that we have come to watch out for: flaming, trolling, bullying, shots fired in the dark.[40] But the feeling of exclusivity that belonged to the early internet, the sense that it belonged

to insiders who knew the secret codes, meant that hostility played a role early on as a gatekeeping measure for
cyberspace. If someone on a forum asked a question that
seemed to give him away as a newcomer, he was flamed
and given fake assistance; the language on the forums was
deliberately aggressive, trip-wired with slang shibboleths
and laced with obscenities—part of the message being,
get out if you can't take the heat.[41] Even the user handles
were meant, in part, as a repellant to outsiders.

Of course, not everyone on the internet was a member
of the Legion of Doom. But using the internet required
some technological savvy: before the World Wide Web
simplified online navigation, users had to navigate using
keyboard commands, and they needed to know the
phone numbers of the servers that hosted the pages they
wanted to view. Well into the 1990s, *cyberspace*, to use a
term that has dropped sharply in popularity with the dis-
solution of the internet's boundaries, was a magic circle.
It required users to develop specialized forms of mastery,
and in exchange it offered young men, in particular, a
protected space in which to enjoy alternative forms of
companionship, authority, status, even masculinity.[42]
They were outsiders, but they were outsiders who were
part of something great.

The belief that this community was under threat
prompted the emergence, in the 1990s, of the earliest
forms of trolling—and, incidentally, the first symbolic use
of the cat as a weapon in the battle over internet culture.

2 THE GREAT LOLCAT MASSACRE

In the early 1990s, commercial entities began taking over the networked world, previously the semisecret domain of hackers, hippies, and hobbyists. Since the 1980s, personal computers had been growing steadily more user-friendly, and the World Wide Web, which Tim Berners-Lee first promoted on Usenet in 1991, gave the internet an easy point-click interface. America Online, CompuServe, Prodigy, and other commercial internet service providers started to sell prepackaged internet connection services, finally recognizing that the time-wasting of internet users had commercial possibilities.

As internet usage spread into the mainstream, general-readership books about "cyberspace" began to appear in bookstores: *Dave Barry in Cyberspace* (1996), *Deeper: My Two-Year Odyssey in Cyberspace* (1997), *My Tiny Life: Crime and Passion in a Virtual World* (1998). These books usually made a point of emphasizing the weirdness of cyberspace—you can find a video of an exploding whale!—and the writer's naïveté about technology.[1] You didn't need specialized knowledge to get online; indeed, new users often made a show of their lack of knowledge when navigating this world. People wore shirts that read, "Roadkill on the Information Superhighway."[2]

This influx seems to have put the boundary maintenance of old communities online under new stress. In his book on exploring cyberspace, John Seabrook describes finding a peculiarly combative tone in much of the talk online. "There is something brutal and predatory about much of what goes on on the Internet," one of his acquaintances said. "There is a kind of smart-ass style one must either learn to ignore, or capture and exploit for one's own purposes." More experienced internet users suggested to Seabrook that that the hostile atmosphere reflected, in part, a reaction against the swarms of newbies entering the forums. One woman he knew, a biologist, wrote to him:

> There is an air of preestablished hierarchy there—if you're new to the Net, or even to a particular group on the Net, you don't belong a priori. As a woman, I have encountered an additional barrier; the net is heavily male and women who want to play with the big boys either have to be ultra tough-talking—"one" of the boys—or else play off as coy, charming, "little-ol-ME?"-feminine. (Even geeks have fantasy lives, I suppose.) Or use a male-neutral alias with no one the wiser.[3]

She added, "For more than a decade these guys had their own secret tin-can-on-a-string way to communicate and socialize, as obscure as ham radio but no pesky FCC requirements and much, much cooler. But then the Internet—their cool secret—started to get press. . . . Imagine these geeks, suddenly afraid that their magic treehouse was about to be boarded by American pop culture. It was worse than having your favorite obscure, underground album suddenly appear on the Billboard charts."[4]

In 1993, an event took place on the Usenet newsgroups that brought together many of the themes that drove early internet culture: the clash between "the internet" and the mainstream, the use of hostility as a form of boundary maintenance, the precarious status of women online. The term that inhabitants of Usenet used for this kind of event was *invasion*: the regulars of one Usenet board descended, en masse, onto another board, posting flames and troll messages.[5] The target of the invasion was a Usenet forum called rec.pets.cats, the regulars of which were largely women; the event was harrowing enough in its intensity, and troubling enough in its implications, for media scholars and journalists to chronicle its course and effects.[6] In disrupting a community of cat lovers, in describing in gruesome detail the torture and execution of cats, the agents of this "invasion" were mounting a protest against the use of the internet by those unlike themselves—which also entailed an attack on femininity, propriety, and dull domesticity. In the scale of the internet's history, the invasion of rec.pets.cats was a minor event. Nonetheless, as an early act of mass trolling whose agents were self-conscious of its status as such, this event offers a view of the processes by which trolling transformed from a niche form of boundary maintenance to a form of harassment endemic to the internet at large. It also affirmed the enduring power of the cat as an instrument of what Darnton calls "symbolic aggression."[7]

In this instance, the hostile force in the invasion was the forum alt.tasteless. In 1990, Usenet administrators had created alt.tasteless as a quarantine board; that is, people who were too disgusting or troublesome for newsgroups like rec.humor were directed to alt.tasteless, where they could exchange dead-baby jokes without bothering civilians.[8] Quarantine boards are still in use today on Facebook and other connective-media platforms, where forums sometimes have split-off forums where users post content too tasteless for the residents of the main forum.[9] Computer game companies are also rumored to use them.[10] However, as the story to follow demonstrates, quarantines have limited effectiveness when trolls work together in groups. (The capacity of trolls in groups to overcome institutional barriers to trolling suggests a reason to conduct more studies of group trolling.)[11]

Within a few years, alt.tasteless had some 60,000 regular readers, as the board's FAQ reported.[12] Contemporary observers seemed to take for granted that most of those readers were male. Certainly, parts of the board's culture suggested a male readership. The readers of alt.tasteless loved to post disgusting facts to gross each other out, and some of their favored gross-out "facts" relied on imaginative ideas about female anatomy.[13]

In 1993, the regulars of alt.tasteless decided to find another newsgroup to invade. Because their mass trolling campaign was an act of boundary maintenance, they had to choose a group of victims who were pointedly unlike themselves. A writer for *Wired* magazine who discussed the event soon afterward understood the gender dynamic at play in their choice, although he communicates this dynamic only implicitly, through choice phrasing:

> One night last summer, the boys on alt.tasteless were feeling, well . . . if it were a Usenet group it might be called alt.restless. Maybe they were getting bored with each other. Maybe they craved the sensation of saying something really gross, and getting a Big Reaction. You know, something sisterly, like EEEEEEEEWWWWW GROOOOOSSSSS! You never get that kind of response on alt.tasteless.
>
> Someone—no one remembers who—suggested invading another Usenet group. A Usenet panty raid! The suggestion was well received by other a.t.'ers. But whom to raid? After much discussion, a likely target emerged:
>
> Rec.pets.cats.[14]

In 1993, the cat had not yet become, in the phrase of journalists, the "spirit animal" of the internet at large. Nonetheless, the choice of cat lovers as targets for this early act of mass trolling was not entirely coincidental. Rec.pets.cats, which dated from 1991, was a forum for trading stories, questions, and tips about cats. The forum's regulars were mostly women, as Stephanie Brail notes. They also happened to be, for the most part, newcomers to the internet and "light" (that is, merely occasional) internet users. They visited Usenet to look up information and to chat with other light users, but not for much else.[15] *Wired* cited a longtime poster in rec.pets.cats as saying that "many of the people in rec.pets.cats are not what you'd describe as typical computer people. We have a lot of unsophisticated users in this group. Many people are steered to the group when they are dealing with the grief of losing a pet, for instance."[16]

For the agents of the invasion, part of the joke—the "metonymic insult," in Darnton's phrase—may well have been the opportunity to play on the cultural trope of the "cat lady": out of touch, ineffectual, undesirable, unable to sustain human relationships and so, to replace those relationships, enamored with pets to the point of obsession.[17] The trope is old: cat owners have a history in popular culture that reaches back from the crazy cat lady to the witch. Stories from the time of witch trials of witches giving suck to their familiars, fawning over them, used the excess of intimacy to evoke disgust, as Barbara Rosen notes: "The element of affection in the alliance, which, on the Continent, took the form of surrender and worship, and bestiality with demons, was in England expressed by the cozy, slightly perverted relationship of a lonely poverty-stricken woman to her pet animal."[18] For the apprentices in Darnton's cat massacre, part of the humor that enlivened the proceedings was the symbolic portrayal of the master's wife as a witch, a portrayal enabled by her keen affection for her cat, *la grise*.[19]

The "panty raid" took the form of spamming the newsgroup with troll posts, which initially posed as serious queries from cat owners. One poster asked what he should do about his cats when he brought dates over, describing their bowel problems and sexual habits in excruciating detail. Another asked how he could kill his girlfriend's cat without her finding out. When the regulars of rec.pets.cats took the bait, the trolling escalated. Invaders posted queries about cooking cats, advice to kill cats with "multiple .357 copper-jacketed hollowpoints," advice to nail cats to boards, and "articles about topics such as vivisecting the cat and having sex with its innards."[20]

In keeping with the practice, borrowed from alt.folklore.urban, of posting shibboleths in or under a troll post that would alert insiders to the prank being played but leave a "trout" in the dark, the trolls in the cat newsgroup sometimes left clues by giving their (imaginary) cats names that corresponded to slang words in their own newsgroup for sexual acts or genitalia.[21] As with slang terms in ordinary language use, the purpose of these clues was to "form a sociolinguistic barrier within which insiders identify themselves through passwords" that outsiders find unfamiliar.[22] This is a behavior that trolls from our own time share, since, as Whitney Phillips has persuasively argued, memes serve as passwords for the users of forums like 4chan, establishing the terms of a shared mental world and its signifiers: "recognizing a meme, remixing a meme, referencing a meme, even simply referencing a meme [helps] to fortify the troll space's . . . subcultural borders."[23] Her emphasis is the sense of triumph that trolls gain by using shared terms from their subculture as weapons against mainstream culture, as when trolls trick mainstream journalists into reciting memes unknowingly. Shibboleths, too, extend the work of boundary maintenance, highlighting the difference between those who understand a term and those who do not.

Another feature that the trolls in the cat newsgroup shared with present-day trolls was a readiness to escalate past the point of mere ridicule. One woman from the cat newsgroup—who took the post about killing a girlfriend's cat seriously and wrote to the police—became the subject of "death threats, hate mail, and harassing phone calls."[24] Another woman, a software engineer, began receiving death threats: "I got mail from people telling me that they wanted to cut me up with knives, that they were going to tie me up and watch me squeal like a pig," she told a reporter. "I got one message where the guy had enclosed my work address."[25]

BOUNDARY MAINTENANCE

In the years since what we might anachronistically call the Great Lolcat Massacre—anachronistically because Lolcats, a major subject of the next chapter, would not emerge on the internet until 2005—the label *trolling* has widened to accommodate many communities, platforms, and behaviors. Few platforms online can claim to have never experienced troll activity; trolls have vandalized Wikipedia pages; flooded Twitter, Facebook, Tumblr, and YouTube feeds with abusive comments; flagged Kickstarter pages for removal; slaughtered their own allies in multiplayer games; and organized distributed denial of service (DDoS) attacks against websites, often focusing on targets who were women or members of other minoritized groups.[26] This is a wide and varied field of activity, and its oft-competing elements highlight an issue that scholars have long struggled with: how to define trolling as a practice.[27] A long historical view can help to establish the concept of boundaries as an important part of that definition. Across communities and platforms today, trolling behaviors continue to assert and, so to speak, militarize the boundaries between in-group and out-group populations in the digital world.

We can even recognize, in hindsight, that the concept of boundaries has been an important component of trolling since the earliest years of the practice. In 1997, the internet scholar Michele Tepper published a study on what was then the novel practice of "trolling," or writing incorrect information online with the hope of being officiously corrected by other internet users.[28] In her article, she takes the stance of a cultural anthropologist documenting an obscure phenomenon that will likely fade as time passes and the internet changes. At the time, few could have suspected how important a phenomenon trolling would become in mainstream culture, both on and off the internet.[29]

Tepper documents the emergence of trolling in the early 1990s in a specific Usenet newsgroup, alt.folklore.urban.[30] This newsgroup, which its regulars called AFU, was devoted to discussing urban legends and confirming or disproving their veracity. (Today, this work is the purview of the website Snopes.com. It may interest readers to know that the two creators of Snopes.com got their start on AFU, where "snopes" was the username of one of the pair.[31] He was, Tepper writes, one of "the two most notorious trollers in AFU.")[32]

Usenet forums were far from the only sites of malicious behavior on the early internet, of course. In 1993, the journalist Julian Dibbell discussed sexual harassment in online text-based virtual communities in his famous article "A Rape in Cyberspace."[33] *Spamming, flaming,* and other terms for online grievances were familiar parlance by that time.[34] But the origin of the specific verb *troll,* and with it the now obsolete noun *troller* (today superseded by the noun *troll*), is worth noting for the clearer view it offers of how the motivations and self-conception of early trolls informed the motivations and self-conception of other hostile online actors, who carried the term *trolling* to other platforms and adopted it with pride as a label for their own behavior.

The practice of trolling arose within AFU because, although the newsgroup had a strong community of regulars, its purpose meant that new people often came in with inane questions or urban legends that the regulars had seen many times and long since disproved. Regulars replied to particularly egregious newbie posts with *even more* egregious misinformation. They also began putting up ridiculous posts meant to catch newbies as soon as they arrived. (Newbie: "You remember incorrectly. Jamie Lee

Curtis was NOT in Star Wars. That was Carrie Fisher."
Troll: "Ridiculous. Carrie Fisher is much too small and
slight to carry that heavy hairy suit around all day on the
set.")[35] The term *trolling* was meant to reference a method
of fishing by letting a line drift with bait.

As Tepper explains, trolling on AFU initially required
subtle irony—an ability to mimic the officious, pedantic
tone of the know-it-all:

> In trolling's Usenet incarnation, the hook is baited with mis-
> information of a specific kind: if it is at first glance incorrect,
> and at a second or third glance comically incorrect, in a
> deliberately comic way, it's probably a good troll. . . . Troll-
> ing requires a certain amount of verbal dexterity . . . and like
> puns, trolls are also most successful if delivered deadpan:
> "Al Capone, who played the heavy on so many Abbott and
> Costello movies, died decades ago, so I doubt he's on *The
> Untouchables*."[36]

When snopes trolled a forum discussion about errors in
Star Trek (he cross-posted to both AFU and the hierarchy
of forums under rec.arts.startrek), his complaint—about
a spaceship throwing a shadow—got the tone just right:
"Hello? Are there any technical advisors working on this
show? Do they really think that objects cast shadows in a
vacuum? I know zip about physics, but even I could spot
that one."[37] His mimicry of internet pedantry is spot-on.

Trolling was a method for the newsgroup to reinforce
its values and guard the community against outsiders,
Tepper argues: "It serves the dual purpose of enforcing
community standards and of increasing community

cohesion by providing a game that all those who know the rules can play against those who do not. It works both as a game and as a method of subcultural boundary demarcation because the playing pieces in this game are not plastic markers or toy money but pieces of information."[38] The newsgroup prided itself on the ability to get information right; it also prided itself on its own history as a community. People who came in and made noise without knowing that history or doing basic research were therefore punished. "The corrector, being outside of the community in which trolling is practiced, believes that he is proving his superiority to the troller by catching the troller's error, but he is in fact proving his inferior command of the codes of the local subculture in which trolling is practiced."[39]

Indeed, AFU regulars dropped hints that a troll *was* a troll by using code words that the "trout" being baited would not recognize. "This ignorance is highlighted within AFU by the group custom of noting in the message header that the post is a troll; acceptable notations include 'troll,' 'llort,' and, as an AFU in-joke, any variation on the phrase 'Phil Gustafson scooped up from lake, scuba gear and all, dropped on forest fire.'"[40] (The phrase refers to an urban legend that, presumably, AFU members grew tired of seeing reposted by newbies who did not know it had long since been debunked.) As we have seen, the invaders of rec.pets.cats engaged in the same practice when they dropped shibboleths that, on their own forum, were crude slang.

On AFU, trolling functioned explicitly as a form of boundary maintenance, having, as it did, the immediate purpose of identifying outsiders and singling them out for the community's ridicule. At the end of a trolling session on AFU, the troll might post an acronym, "YHBT. YHL. HAND" ("You Have Been Trolled. You Have Lost. Have A Nice Day"), that, as Tepper notes, "in its very unintelligibility mocks the catch's outsider status." (AFU regulars joked that the acronym should be "WAFU, YN," or "We're alt.folklore.urban, you're not.")[41] In its function as a form of boundary maintenance, the practice of trolling illustrates the importance, for self-identified internet insiders, of maintaining an identity separate from that of the world at large.

As a technique for policing the boundaries of a community of self-identified internet insiders—in the initial instance, that of an internet newsgroup—trolling was quickly understood to be adaptable for use in other communities, even though the performative stance that it relied on, the stance of the condescending, confident, and thoroughly incorrect self-appointed authority on a given subject, was perhaps especially recognizable in a community dedicated to adjudicating urban legends, internet rumors, and what came, much later, to be described as "fake news." The AFU forum's FAQ discouraged trolling in other newsgroups—"if you must troll, bear in mind that trolling outside of AFU is pretty weak"—but people did it anyway. One AFU regular who wrote in favor of trolling other forums described the members of those forums as "foreigners" and "the filthy masses."[42] By these lights, trolling is what you do to outsiders, to foreigners, to filthy casuals, regardless of where you may find them online; you use it to punish them for not being insiders and to play a secret game of inclusion with your own community.

Perhaps those who shared this insider perspective already foresaw what some onlookers missed, which is that trolling would continue to thrive even as most obvious "outsiders" online, namely novices to the "Internet Superhighway," faded as a presence in the online world. Writing in the late 1990s, Tepper suggested that trolling would soon die out as a practice, since the population of internet users was growing so quickly that the mainstream should soon overtake the internet's old subcultures: "As the promise of the Information Superhighway continues to gain in popularity, more people with little previous background in computing are thrown into a preexisting culture with rules they might not understand. As Usenet continues to change, trolling will probably become less and less effective as a community-formation technique."[43]

More than two decades later, we can see that the opposite happened. Trolling became a familiar practice in every corner of the internet; in the process, it became more vicious, less purposeful, and less artful—an undirected attack on anyone who belonged (in the infinitely flexible phrase) to the filthy masses. Though scholars express uncertainty as to whether trolling is an established norm of behavior online, they concede that in gaming communities, at least, players are expected to treat *encountering* trolls as a normal experience: "It is clear that trolling is considered a negative phenomenon, but it is also an expected phenomenon, a 'rite of passage.'"[44] The invasion of rec.pets.cats, which was a self-conscious act of group trolling, represented an early example of this kind of harassment. In tearing apart a community of cat lovers, in describing in gruesome detail the torture and execution of cats, they were mounting a protest against the use of the internet by those unlike themselves. A team-building blitzkrieg. A panty raid.

Ultimately, the cat massacre that took place on Usenet in 1993 can usefully be seen as an event that the agents who brought it about purposefully made exemplary. The cultures of trolling that later grew and flourished in the forums of Something Awful and 4chan borrowed more from the playbook of alt.tasteless and similar communities than from the more temperate, even artful, trolls of alt.folklore.urban. But an understanding of the reactivity to outsiders that these communities shared can help us to better appreciate what was at stake in the Lolcat Massacre and similar events. The pranks that constituted early trolling were not, as some scholars later suggested, acts of undirected aggression, chaos, or trickery, but rather represented a purposeful game that, like the semiotic warfare of early hacker communities, sought through aggression to police boundary regions in the online world.

Just to be clear, I am not suggesting that hacker communities on the early internet belonged to the same population as trolls; only that the feeling of exclusivity that belonged to the early internet, the sense that it belonged to insiders who knew the secret codes, meant that boundary maintenance, the identification of in-group members and rejection of out-group members, was a major concern of communities of self-identified insiders, of which the behavior of both hacker communities and early troll forums offer potent examples.

The event also extended a long tradition of finding recreation in the ceremonial rejection of people who could be associated with cats, though the identity of those people has changed many times over the centuries: heretics, papists, cuckolds, witches, women, and others. Given punk culture's propensity for choosing identity markers that belong to low and vilified domains—as I have noted, even the word *punk* originally meant a sex worker, a bad woman—perhaps it was only a matter of time before a community of self-identified internet insiders chose these weird, wayward animals as their mascot.

3   EXTREMELY ONLINE FELINES

Few new-media practices have spread through the world entire at the moment of their creation. When I was in college in the 2000s, I traded emails regularly with a friend in another state. We never once exchanged memes, because we didn't know they existed. Already, down in the seventh circle of the internet, memes—a term that refers to a genre of internet content, especially image macros, or images with superimposed captions, that is meant to be revised, remixed, and shared—had arisen in an image-board subculture whose roots lay in anonymity, participatory culture, remixing, and dark humor.[1] But they were still underground; my friend sometimes sent messages that gave text captions to pictures of cute animals, but she came up with this practice, an imitation of captioned postcards and newspaper photographs, on her own. Years later, when memes finally caught the attention of the world at large, they permanently changed internet culture. And with them came the endless summer of the cat.

This chapter explores the significance of cats in the subcultures that helped to set down the social protocols of Web 2.0. The communities that laid the social foundations of meme culture saw themselves as inhabitants of the periphery as opposed to the mainstream; the ascendance of the cat as the mascot of the internet relied on a view of the internet as a snarky, alienated alternative to the mainstream. These communities included many Americans who were fascinated with Japanese culture, which further drove the popularity of cat memes on their boards. Lolcats, the image macros that introduced meme culture to the mainstream, ultimately derive, through 4chan, from the Japanese forum 2chan; meme culture itself has deep roots in *japonisme*.

THE IMAGEBOARD SUBCULTURE

In 1999, Hiroyuki Nishimura, a 22-year-old entrepreneur in Tokyo, created a bulletin board named 2channel. Within a few years, it had become the most popular website in Japan. Nishimura modeled the board after an earlier bulletin board, Ayashii World ("Strange World"), which ran on Usenet from 1996 to 1998 and devoted itself to tech-underground pursuits like hacking. The mainstream success of 2channel was the result of good timing combined with a suite of social and technological protocols from Ayashii World that emphasized anonymity and freedom.[2] "It's become one of the few places where Japanese people can say exactly what they feel without concern for decorum or propriety," *Wired* magazine later said of Nishimura's site. "On 2channel, anyone can start a thread and anyone can post—there's no need to register or log in and no Web handles. There are no censors, no filters, no age verification, no voting systems that boost one thread or comment over another."[3]

Discussion threads on 2channel run heavy on snide remarks, juvenile banter, slang, and inside jokes, many observers have noted.[4] Notably, for our purposes, 2channel popularized the use of internet-born images as local inside jokes and local mascots: predecessors of memes. On text-only bulletin boards, these images consisted of ASCII art. Many early 2channel memes were ASCII representations of cats, which the board's users gave distinctive names and personalities. Following what became the fundamental moves of play in meme culture, users would copy-paste these figures from one location to another, in the process adding or changing elements—for instance, adding the speech caption *itte yoshi*, or "get lost."[5]

A bulletin-board aficionado writing in 2004, after 2channel had become established as Japan's most popular website, described some of the board's more popular figures:

Mona, a mixture of a cat and a bear; the informal mascot of 2channel.

```
~´  ——(°д°)
  UU    U U
```

A cat named Giko (or Giko-neko, meaning "Giko cat"); migrated to 2channel from another bulletin board.

Fusa-Giko, or "wooly" Giko: a fuzzy cat.

Shii, a female cat in a box.

Onigiri, a cat with a rice cake on his head.

```
オマエモナー
```

Fusa-Mona, or "wooly" Mona: another fuzzy cat.

A cat named Nida; understood to be a version of Mona from Korea. Users often pasted in ASCII art of knives and guns attacking this character.

A cat named Morara, a playmate of Mona's.

A character named Hikki, of unknown species; represents "depression."

Zonu, a dog; represents "unaccountability."[6]

The cats of 2channel extended an antique fascination with cats in Japanese culture.[7] In Japan, shopkeepers and restaurateurs commonly place figurines of cats with beckoning paws, called *maneki-neko*, at their doorways for good luck. Cat colonies are often allowed to live near Shinto shrines, and Buddhist tradition says that cats were once entrusted with guarding scriptures from mice. According to folklore, cats can bring good or bad fortune at will, and the unfortunate person who kills a cat will be reborn with bad luck for seven lifetimes. During the Edo period, owners supposedly killed their cats when the cats turned seven, lest the cats take on demonic features and turn on their owners.[8]

Magical cats have abounded in Japanese media for centuries (as in the anime *Sailor Moon*, where cats serve as supernatural guardians). In the 18th century, artists who depicted the "floating world" of Tokyo often included cats in their images, gazing out of windows or playing at the feet of ladies; one historian writes, "It is hard to find an artist of the period who didn't sneak a cat in somewhere." In 1842, when new laws came down that outlawed prints of kabuki actors and geisha, artists began to sell, as a clever workaround, prints of cats wearing clothing and living it up as actors, geisha, and other denizens of the floating world. The artist Utagawa Kuniyoshi became especially famous for a corpus of prints that suggested that Tokyo's nightlife concealed a secret society of supernatural shape-shifting cats.[9] Today, these images have inspired dozens of news pieces about antique "Japanese Lolcats."[10]

Even the kanji, or character, for cat has origins in the supernatural. During the Asuka period, or around the mid-6th to the mid-7th centuries, stories began to circulate about a demonic creature called the *mikeneko* (creature with three colors of fur), which could be identified by its "fiery eyes." In rural areas, people told stories of catlike creatures who walked on two legs; of felines that could fly, known as *kasha*, shameless thieves of bodies from cemeteries; of enormous felines with two tails, known as *nekomata*, that hunted travelers in the forest. In the Japanese language, the word *neko* came to indicate cats; *mikeneko* now means "calico cat."[11]

Incidentally, the word *emoji*, a term that refers to a single-character pictogram in a digital message, derives from the Japanese words *e* ("picture") and *moji* ("character").[12] In the English-speaking world, emojis are a fairly recent phenomenon, having become standard on Apple devices in 2011, on Windows devices between 2012 and 2015, and on Android phones in 2013. In Japan, consumers could use emojis starting in the 1990s, when the telecom provider NTT DoCoMo made them available on internet-connected cell phones. The first set of emojis, 176 in total, included a whiskered, smiling cat.[13]

In 2003, Christopher Poole, a 15-year-old coder living in upstate New York, decided to create an English-speaking version of 2channel and its imageboard spinoff, 2chan. When he browsed these sites, he had to follow the pictures, since he spoke no Japanese—but he liked what he saw. Poole wanted a site, like 2chan, that would update constantly with new content; as for the tone, he hoped to emulate the eclectic grotesqueries of sites like 2chan, Futaba Channel (another Japanese bulletin board), and Something Awful, a website that both lampooned and celebrated the weirdest, nerdiest, most outrageous content that could be found on the web.[14] Collaborating with a programmer he had met on the forums of Something Awful, he combined new software with code he cabbaged from Futaba Channel to build the imageboard 4chan.net. Poole first advertised 4chan on a Something Awful forum, for anime enthusiasts, called Anime Death Tentacle Rape Whorehouse.[15]

The name of that forum was a joke, of course: a parody of the outside world's perception of anime fans and of the excesses that anime fans knew lurked on some of their boards. It also reflected the comedic style of Something Awful, and indeed the comedic style of many other web communities in its wake, from 4chan to Weird Twitter to Vine: whimsical, snarky, despairing, grotesque, self-reflexively obsessed with the lowest-energy state of new media.[16] The appeal of Something Awful, a former administrator of the site told a journalist, was its comedic attention to the worst of internet culture—for instance, essays in the voice of a character who was "a parody of a really shitty teenager who was just getting on the internet for the first time, being really adamant about all of his shitty opinions."[17]

On the other hand, the phrase *anime death tentacle rape whorehouse* is ... a lot. The shock humor that prevailed on this forum and others like it—including, in time, the forums of 4chan—functioned, in part, as a form of gatekeeping: if you didn't like the jokes, you didn't belong there. The house style of Something Awful—especially the site's main page, which set the tone for the forums— caught the attention of a specific demographic, as one onlooker noted: the "dark, esoteric humor proved popular among a certain set—typically young, typically male, often though not always left-leaning."[18] The style of humor on 4chan likewise proved attractive to a specific demographic: young, male, rebellious—and, as the years passed, increasingly to the right, as political events forced a growing divide between the left and right sides of libertarianism within the United States.[19]

POST SOME FUCKING CATS! IT'S CATURDAY!

Although 4chan began as a community for enthusiasts of manga and anime, it soon became a place to exchange images and chatter relating to current events, food, origami, "otaku culture," *mecha* (robots), paranormal phenomena, Pokémon, technology, television, video games, and many other subjects. (And pornography. A lot of pornography.)[20] As an imageboard, it trafficked primarily in images; and as a community designed for fans, it nurtured forms of media consumption that, as scholars of participatory culture have extensively shown, differed from the forms of reading that academic criticism enshrines.[21] On 4chan, anime fans could find bootleg copies of shows; share obscure content; trade fan theories; discuss lore; or share original artwork, costumes, or writing.[22] They imported many images directly from 2chan, along with certain conventions for recycling and remixing content.

Finding exact dates in 4chan's history can be a challenge, since the site does not save old content and the Internet Archive does not crawl its pages. But sometime around 2005, 4chan's /b/ ("random") board started a weekly tradition of posting cute cat pictures on Saturday, a tradition that users called "Caturday." Part of the humor of Caturday came from the contrast between cute cats and the board's "usual stream of gross-out content."[23] The weekly posts that inaugurated Caturday threads were often aggressive and profane, as though to suggest that only a shield of hostility could protect the posters from the tender aura of the pictures: "CATURDAY. Post some fucking cats!" "CATURDAY, BITCHES." "IT'S CATURDAY. Yiff in hell, furfags."[24] (The threads that followed were equally coarse.)

In 2006, the community began to circulate cat pictures in the form of image macros. A set of conventions for these image macros fell into place: the captions are in the first person (that is, the cats supposedly write the captions themselves); the captions use phonetic spelling (since most cats lack a formal education); and the captions use a garbled dialect that 4chan users, always ready to stretch a joke, continually regularized, so that today—for instance—we can say with the authority of a linguist that Lolcats, like children, "over-regularize" the endings of irregular verbs. (The plural of *eat* is *eated*, not *ate*.)[25] Someone gave this genre of image macro the name *Lolcats*, and the name stuck. ("LOL" is a texting abbreviation meaning "laughing out loud.")

Cole Stryker sums up the appeal of Lolcats as follows: "Here's the idea: A humorous photo of a cat accompanied by a caption written in a pidgin English derived from rushed IM speak. The stupidly funny broken English coupled with the inherent cuteness of the cat images made for a viral phenomenon. Lolcats were dumb, catchy, and approachable enough that anyone could pick up on the humor after seeing a few."[26]

In the early days, when Lolcats circulated mostly on 4chan, Fark, and Something Awful, they tended to use edgy or raunchy humor. One popular meme showed a cat peering down from a missing ceiling tile, together with the caption, "Ceiling cat is watching you masturbate." Really, anything that produced humor by setting raunch against cute had good odds for success on these sites, Lolcat or no. Another meme that took off on Fark was an image of two Domo-kun (monsters that serve as mascots for a Japanese television station) chasing a kitten, with the caption, "Every time you masturbate, God kills a kitten. Please, think of the kittens."[27] (When I was in college, one dormitory had an all-male hall that students had nicknamed "the monastery." Residents of the monastery wore T-shirts that bore the same image of two Domo-kun chasing a kitten, now with the caption, "Another one bites the dust.")

Why Lolcats should become the best-known meme on the internet—a meme familiar even to internet users who don't know what memes are—is a question worth asking because that very popularity suggests that significantly different demographics find something relatable, or at least *legible*, in the meme's sensibility. One part of that sensibility is the pairing of cuteness and aggression, which the genre retained though it lost its raunchiness outside of the communities in which it began. Another part, which has likewise remained consistent across the many platforms and communities that circulate Lolcats, is the constructed language of Lolcats ("lolspeak").

The premise of lolspeak is that cats have picked up English but only superficially, so they use phonetic spelling and make errors common to speakers who haven't learned the language's irregularities; but, more than this, that cats are internet addicts who are fluent in the slang and in-jokes of new media. Some observers describe lolspeak in terms of "rushed IM speak": the lexicon of slang, abbreviations, and common misspellings that people use when sending texts and instant messages (*you* becomes *u*).[28] Others note the presence of idioms from hacker boards and gaming communities (*haxxor, pwn, teh*).[29] I also suspect that, in its odd phrasing and improper syntax (especially its improper subject-verb agreement), lolspeak riffs on the new-media genre of *Japanglish*: the stilted translations from Japanese that the users of Fark and 4chan encountered while growing up in toys, anime, and video games. The brand name *Game Boy* is deliberate Japanglish, as are *Walkman* and *Hello Kitty*.[30] Memorable examples of accidental Japanglish have become internet memes: for instance, "A winner is you," from the 1987 game *Pro Wrestling*, and "All your base are belong to us," from the 1992 game *Zero Wing*.[31]

COOL JAPAN

In fact, Japan provided many of the aesthetics, the cultural politics, and the social traditions that made the cat, for Western digerati of the early 21st century, such a resonant and relatable sign. In the final decades of the 20th century, Japan had fascinated observers in the West as the symbol of an alternative modernity. In the 1980s, when many users of 4chan and Something Awful had been children, Western visions of the future registered fear and awe at what politicians described as the "Japanese miracle": an extraordinary rate of economic growth, sustained year after year, accompanied by global domination in the manufacture of automobiles and consumer electronics. Japan had become a superpower not through military might, but through technological and economic dominance, as Douglas McGray, who created the phrase "Gross National Cool," remarked.[32] In Hollywood films set in the future, which increasingly drew on the new genre of *cyberpunk*, references to Asia abounded: *Alien* (1979), where the spaceship that carries the heroes is the property of a Japanese corporation; *Blade Runner* (1982), where the hero eats at a sushi stand, bathed in a color that one of the film's employees called "Asian Blade Runner Blue," while, high in the city above, a video billboard displays the smiling face of a geisha; *The Matrix* (1999), where characters face off in anime-style fight scenes and move through vertical showers of source code that blend numerals with kanji.[33] If Paris had been the capital of the 19th century, Tokyo was the capital of the future.

During these years, Japan also produced a growing share of the popular culture of young Americans. Americans grew up playing Japanese video games (*Mario Brothers, Resident Evil, Street Fighter*); watching anime television shows (*Sailor Moon, Transformers*) and live-action shows that refigured Japanese predecessors (*The Mighty Morphin Power Rangers*); reading manga (*Inuyasha*); buying Japanese collectibles (*Hello Kitty*); and using Japanese electronics (Nintendo Gameboy, Sony Playstation, Tamagotchi, Walkman). Many of these properties expanded across multiple media verticals, pioneering the practice, now ubiquitous in American popular culture, of transmedia storytelling.[34] Pokémon, which started as a video game in 1996, had by 2000 become "a media-mix empire of Game Boy game, comic, cartoon, movies, cards, and toy merchandise."[35] Even after the Japanese economy softened in the 1990s, Japan's domination of American media continued to grow.[36] In 2002, the *New Yorker* published a cover image that made redundant a decades-long critical discussion of "techno-orientalism": a woodblock-style illustration of a Japanese woman wearing a kimono made of Pikachu pelts, using earphone wires to decorate her traditional high-bun hairstyle, and brandishing a fan made of mobile phones.[37]

In fact, these media properties were a subject of Japanese foreign policy.[38] Drawing on a heavily cited article that McGray wrote for the journal *Foreign Policy* in 2002, which argued that Japan could sustain its position as a superpower even during an economic recession through the "soft power" of its cultural influence (what McGray called Japan's "Gross National Cool"), Japan's government instituted a policy, termed "Cool Japan," of promoting the export of Japanese popular culture.[39]

To this day, internet culture in the United States registers an enthrallment with Japanese popular culture that some observers have called *japonisme*, a term that refers to a rage for Japanese art that took over the art world in England, France, and the United States in the late 19th century.[40] Japonisme in American web communities has left profound marks on the aesthetics of computer culture. One such mark is a preference for simplicity in design, argues Christine Yano, who notes that we can find in both centuries-old Japanese illustrations and contemporary icons such as Hello Kitty a style of depicting faces, known as *hikime-kagihana*, that entails "abstracting a face through shorthand stylistic symbols"—which artists developed to help the viewer identify with the subject, or perhaps to allow the viewer to project onto the subject a range of emotions.[41] The repertoire of simplicity to which this style belongs, she argues, joins traditional Japanese art with "computer-mediated and text-messaging practices of *kaomoji* (emoticons)."[42]

Another such mark is a fascination with visual idioms that foreground two-dimensional space—idioms which abound in anime, manga, and early video games. For example, the popular internet character Nyan Cat, which an American twentysomething created in 2011, uses a two-dimensional style as part of its riff on Japanese pop idioms. (Nyan Cat, which grooves to the music of the virtual singer Hatsune Miku, takes its name from the Japanese word *nya*, the equivalent of *meow*.)

Readers interested in Japanese analyses of these idioms should check out the Japanese Neo Pop movement of the 1990s and Takashi Murakami's "Superflat" movement of the 2000s, which, in dialogue with the Cool Japan policy, played with the forms of consumer pop culture in order to critique them.[43] Taking cues from American pop art, the artists who contributed to these movements riffed on the way that global consumer culture made Japanese culture (in the term of the media scholar Koichi Iwabuchi) *odorless*: reproducible, remixable, universally consumable; "Something that could be copied the world over, and everybody could like."[44] In his "Super Flat Manifesto" (2000), Murakami described flatness in terms of the simplification entailed in merging cultural spheres, repackaging cultures for the global marketplace, or creating universally usable digital interfaces: "One way to imagine super flatness is to think of the moment when, in creating a desktop graphic for your computer, you merge a number of distinct layers into one. . . . I would like you, the reader, to experience the moment when the layers of Japanese culture, such as pop, erotic pop, otaku, and H.I.S.-ism [cheap travel to the West], fuse into one."[45] Later, he wrote: "So what is 'super flat'? The words denote a flattened surface, the working environment of computer graphics, flat-panel monitors, or the forceful integration of data into an image. The flat reality left when Pop fizzled; a flattened, self-mocking culture."[46]

THE EMPIRE OF CUTE

The aesthetics of contemporary internet culture include several strands which often weave together. One is weirdness—what the meme scholars Whitney Phillips and Ryan Milner call "the presumption of the weirdness of digital content," which they connect, with no further explanation, with the commonplace saying that "the internet is made of cats."[47] Another is what the media critic Nick Douglas calls "internet ugly," a defiantly lo-fi style of content that nostalgically evokes older media, uses hasty creation as a point of pride, and perhaps carries a residue from the aesthetic of punk zines—an aesthetic that Dick Hebdige calls an "overwhelming impression of urgency and immediacy, of a paper produced in indecent haste, of memos from the front line."[48] A third is cuteness—and this strand, the proliferation of cute kitties, sparkly unicorns, and big-eyed selfies, shares important themes with the legacy of punk in the hacker underground. For youth culture in Japan is as saturated with cute style as American youth culture is saturated with punk style; like punk style, cute style is political.[49] Cute style in Japan, as one scholar explains, figures childhood as counterculture, rebellion as a state of play:

> Cute style is anti-social; it idolizes the pre-social. By immersion in the pre-social world, otherwise known as childhood, cute fashion blithely ignores or outrightly contradicts values central to the organization of Japanese society and the maintenance of the work ethic. By acting childish, Japanese youth try to avoid the conservatives' moral demand that they

exercise self-discipline (*enryō*) and responsibility (*sekinin*) and tolerate (*gaman*) severe conditions (*kurō, kudō*) whilst working hard (*doryoku*) in order to repay their obligation (*giri, on*) to society. Rather than working hard, cuties seem to just want to play and ignore the rest of society completely.[50]

Westerners rebel by acting like teenagers; in Japan, one rebels by acting childlike. For this reason, the American internet's embrace, as part of its "millennial *japonisme*," of Japan's culture of cute fits the countercultural politics that already pervade the world of new media.[51]

The forms of cuteness that the internet embraces—for example, Grumpy Cat and Lil Bub, internet-famous cats with physical deformities—often correspond more precisely with the Japanese aesthetics of *kawaii* than with the Anglo-American aesthetics of *cute*.[52] (Kawaii is a notoriously complex word, but for our purposes we might translate it as "vulnerable and cute."[53] One magazine has called it "the most widely used, widely loved, habitual word in modern living Japanese.")[54] Figures that viewers identify as kawaii often exhibit a flaw that complicates their beauty and deepens their impression of vulnerability. Physical disability, for instance; or they might be "socially deformed," as with the Neo Pop artist Nara Yoshitomo's images of angry, angsty, maladjusted little girls.[55]

WEIRD JAPAN

If the trope, common today among both media scholars and lay internet users, that online spaces are cauldrons of "transglobal weirdness," reflects (in part) the celebration of Japanese media on American internet forums in the 1990s and 2000s, that celebration also framed Japanese media in terms congruent with a belief that online spaces should be weird.[56] Representations of Japan often emphasized the weirdness of Japanese culture: sometimes this trope entailed imagining Japan as an exotic alternate world, and sometimes it entailed an "ironic consumption" of texts—as *cheesy*—that seemed fanciful or absurd in their racial otherness.[57] For the members of *extremely online* communities, who used a shared media language to constitute themselves as a population distinct from others, circulating images of Weird Japan served, in part, to signal membership in an imagined community of weirdos.

The Americans who passionately circulated Japanese media often described themselves as *otaku*. American nerds borrowed the term from Japan, where it arose in the 1980s as a derisive term for young men obsessed with anime, technology, and video games; in the West, otaku came to mean someone obsessed with Japanese pop culture, or indeed with Japanese culture at large.[58] Despite the term's unfavorable connotations in Japanese media, Westerners took it up, one scholar notes, as "a badge of honor among fans."[59] The media scholar Matt Hills suggests that Western otaku chose their derisive label deliberately to celebrate their status as outcasts and misfits.[60]

One of the first celebrity animals on the internet became a celebrity largely because of the trope of "weird Japan." In 2001, Syberpunk, a little-known English-language personal blog that focused on gaming and movies, posted several images of a rabbit with odd items balanced atop his head: bread, a teacup, dorayaki (which resemble pancakes). The rabbit's name was Oolong; the images came from the blog of the rabbit's owner, Hironori Akutagawa of Hokkaido.[61] The rabbit went *viral*, in a term new to the web.[62] As the Syberpunk blog was barraged with traffic from people looking for pictures of Oolong, the blog's writer posted angrily about how much money he suddenly had to pay for server costs, then took down the pictures of Oolong and told visitors to go elsewhere, then closed the blog and reopened it as a "repository of all things strange and uniquely Japanese."[63] The new site's homepage featured an image of Oolong.

Oolong, in the meanwhile, moved through the new stations of internet fame: a *nom de meme* ("Pancake bunny," "Oolong the pancake rabbit"); a mention in the *New York Times*; rebirth as an image macro with a snarky caption: "I have no idea what you're talking about . . . so here's a bunny with a pancake on its head."[64]

THE LOLCAT EMPIRE

On January 11, 2007, a user posted a meme to Something Awful showing a fat gray cat with an open-mouthed look of happy anticipation. It bore the caption: "I Can Has Cheezburger?" The style of the meme—the cat, the broken English, the Impact font—drew upon 4chan's Caturday festivities.[65]

A woman in Hawaii named Kari Unebasami sent the meme from Something Awful to her friend, Eric Nakagawa, to cheer him up after a bad day. He liked it so much that he started a blog dedicated to replicating the joke: a one-stop shop for cats with captions. The blog was so popular that when Nakagawa hotlinked an image from the website of a computer maven named Ben Huh, keeping the image digitally connected to its server of origin, the traffic from Nakagawa's site caused Huh's server to crash.[66] Huh tracked down Nakagawa and contacted him to tell him to stop, and to make the story short, they went into business together.

The site's visitors—ordinary civilians who found Lolcats appealing but were in no way prepared to visit 4chan to find them—created, submitted, followed, and shared images of Lolcats as a form of playbor. Eventually Huh bought the site, seeing potential for purr-izontal spread. "The blog was already hugely popular," the historian William Stryker writes, "but Huh spun the thing into a network of meme-oriented blogs that had the sort of numbers major newspapers would envy, with the flagship site achieving over ten million daily hits."[67]

Yet Lolcats, having caught the attention of the general public at precisely the moment that the general public decided to learn about memes, remained a core symbol with which the public made meaning of the web's new ways of making meaning. Bookstores sold Lolcat treasuries, Lolcat self-help books, and a Lolcat translation of the Bible.[68] A Lolcats musical appeared off-Broadway.[69] Dozens of newspaper and magazine articles that set out to discuss the world of memes started by discussing Lolcats, presumably because general readers would have seen them.[70] "If I come across someone who's never heard of Internet memes," Stryker writes, "the first thing I usually say is, 'Have you ever seen Lolcats?' That's because it's not only the biggest thing to come out of 4chan, it's the undisputed biggest Internet meme."[71]

In 2011, Kate Miltner, the author of a master's thesis on Lolcats for the London School of Economics, found that many of the users who frequented the forums on I Can Has Cheezburger—they referred to themselves as "cheez-frenz"—were "older women" who found the forums to be a community for those who (as one said) "want to be nice, want to be happy, want to give support, want to smile."[72] They shared more cat memes with family and friends, they said, than with strangers on the internet; the in-joke intimacy of meme culture could reinforce real-life companionability. Even so, for these users, too, cats could channel a dark emotional spectrum: Lolcats allowed Miltner's subjects "to laugh at their own foibles, but also express emotions that might otherwise be seen as 'unacceptable' for any number of reasons."[73] The image macros on the Cheezburger network show cats brooding over cups of coffee, yowling at unwanted company, and struggling with window blinds while complaining (via text overlay) about marriage.

Perhaps the semiotic sadness of cats, the dark themes they make available to us, is the feature that enabled Lolcats to make the leap from underground internet subcultures to the internet community at large—to be the butt of a joke that many demographics of internet users understood and found to be funny.[74] We like dogs to be simple and find depictions of dogs that are not happy and loyal disturbing; we allow cats to be complicated—grumpy, goofy, imperious, moody—because we have learned that it's acceptable to take pleasure in their displeasure.

When Lolcats went mainstream, the communities that created Lolcats responded with scorn. One meme lord whom Miltner interviewed said the Lolcat trend ended, as far as he was concerned, once his mother started sending them.[75] In 2008, Something Awful ran a satirical article titled "Internet Cats Are a Hoot and a Half," a parody of an out-of-touch middle-aged woman who had just discovered Lolcats. The supposed author, a woman named Luann, writes, "Anybody who reads my column knows that I love two things equally above everything else, even chocolate: my husband Darryl and cats. Kitties. Cutie babies. Whatever y'all want to call them they are the light of my life." She continues:

> Socrates I think said that laughter is the best medicine, but when y'all are havin' the sorta Monday I am having then laughter can be in short supply. Thankfully, I have found a cure that brings plenty of laughs and it turns out it also helps with one of the other issues I discussed ...
>
> "Lolcats" it's called. That's short for Laughing Out Loud Cats. No, the cats aren't the ones laughing, but you will be!

A Lolcat is what you get when you take a picture of a cat (or sometimes other animals!) making a funny face or getting into all sorts of mischief. Then you put a funny message in "Lolcat speak" onto the image. It's sort of like baby talk and it is really funny. It's the way a cat might talk if he or she could!

Since part of the joke is that Luann enjoys "Laughing Out Loud Cats" without knowing of their history in terrifying internet subcultures, she recommends ICanHasCheez burger.com and Lolcats.com as the main "places on the Internet for you to get Lolcats." She closes by remarking that a reader of her column sent her a video that she expects will be as much fun as Lolcats—which the readers of Something Awful would recognize as a video of an accident that brutally damages a man's rectum: "A Luannatic has e-mailed me something called 'ıguyıjar' and I am really looking forward to checking that one out. If it's a whole lot of fun and a whole lot of funny, you can be sure Luann will bring it to you."[76]

From the satire's point of view, Luann would be more justified in enjoying funny pictures of cats if she did it according to the traditional methods: by dropping into 4chan, browsing a Caturday thread, and writing comments like "remain hidden, faggot" and "kill it with fire." Or by posting a Photoshopped transformation of Happy Cat in a Photoshop thread on Something Awful. But performing the ritual of meme creation without being in the priesthood—writing in "baby talk" without learning the intricacies of lolspeak—affronted the mastery that meme lords had achieved through immersion in the web's in-jokes.[77] And enjoying a meme outside of its original ecosystem threatened the distinctive identity belonging to self-identified internet insiders, even if the basis of that enjoyment was similar for every audience: the way that cats can channel both happy and angry messages, can represent both the alienated self and the alienated other.

By now, however, the cat was out of the bag. In the participatory culture of Web 2.0, cats proved to be a joke with staying power: a symbol of internet culture that in a single picture, GIF, or six-second video could tap into a cascade of stereotypes about the online world: its weirdness, the antisocial reputation of its denizens, its love of cuteness, its love of cheesiness, its japonisme, its nostalgia for media from the 1980s and 90s, its superficiality, its anger, the terrible things we share about ourselves online.[78]

PURR·TICIPATORY CULTURE

In 2018, a girl named Emilie Chang posted to a cat appreciation group on Facebook a picture of a veterinarian's weight chart for cats, with the chunkiest cat given a new label that said, "OH LAWD HE COMIN."[79] The meme went viral on Twitter and, following the "memetic logics" of participatory culture, quickly began to inspire new creations and mashups based on the image and phrase.[80] A Twitter user posted a photo of a strutting chunky cat with the caption, "i can feel he comin in the air tonight / oh lawd."[81] (This tweet went viral, too.) Another Twitter user posted a photo of *un gros chat* strutting past the Eiffel Tower, with the caption, "Oh lawd il vient." An artist on DeviantArt, a portfolio site for user-generated art, posted a digital painting of an enormous cat, apparently based on the cat in the "comin in the air tonight" tweet, standing astride a mountain range, his whiskers level with the clouds.[82] New-media scholars such as Henry Jenkins have, since the 1990s, discussed the transformative texts that fans make of mainstream media properties—fan art, fan fiction, fanzines—but this was fan art of a tweet. It was a signal that participatory culture had, to borrow a conceit, entered its Baroque period: perpetually referential, with each text leading to others which led to others still, disorienting in its subversion of the idea of a dominant text, frame, or interpretation.[83]

When the *Harvard Business Review* described social activity, in 1986, as a "surprising property of computing," it meant to describe people's inclination to waste time as an unwelcome side effect of computer networks in the business world.[84] In the decades after, that inclination would prove to be one of the most socially transformative—and monetizable—aspects of the new technology. Internet cats not only helped to label the social internet, in all its weirdness, its hostility, and its "memetic processes," but also, by joining the internet at large in a shared canonical formulation, a shared symbol that different online cultures could send and receive across their boundaries, provided a key term for discussing the social internet, participating in it, and negotiating the boundaries within it.[85] In the case of the meme

"OH LAWD HE COMIN," memetic iterations of the phrase on Twitter began to attract criticism because the phrase is African-American Vernacular English and many of the people using it were not African Americans. On December 18, 2018, the Monterey Bay Aquarium in Monterey, California, tweeted a photo of a chunky otter with the caption, "Abby is a thicc girl/ What an absolute unit/ She c h o n k/ Look at the size of this lady/ OH LAWD SHE COMIN/ Another Internetism!" The tweet went viral; but the delighted remarks of commenters and reposters soon gave way to a serious conversation about the corporate Twitter account's appropriation of slang (*thicc*) and syntax ("she comin", with its copula deletion) from African-American communities. The aquarium apologized for the tweet the next day.[86]

As Adrienne Massanari writes, discussions of participatory culture in both academia and the media have often "exaggerated the democratic potential and minimized the actual contradictions that it embodies." The offline and online communities that produce and circulate the texts of participatory culture do not work as unmarked agents within an unmarked knowledge-commons but rather construct themselves, as we have seen, with and against other communities.[87] The democratic openness of participatory platforms to admit new contributions from any quarter, or to allow different quarters to borrow content from each other, can set off turf wars, as when the denizens of Something Awful derided, through Luann, the spread of Lolcats into parts of the internet that the general public frequented (and, by extension, the spread of the internet into the homes and offices of the general public). Or again, this openness can devalue the distinctive idioms of minoritized groups, for instance by causing a real-world language variant to seem, to those without much exposure to it, like just another instance of the internet's weirdness. (Recently, the Alan Turing Institute published a study of the website Urban Dictionary that entirely ignored the website's origins in, and extensive use of, the slang lexicon of African Americans. To the European scholars who wrote the study, the language of Urban Dictionary evidently sounded "informal, unfamiliar," *internetty*, but did not suggest a real-world speech community.)[88]

Ultimately, the canon of internettiness for which internet cats serve as the figurehead continues to inform the development of the internet as a social institution. On the microlevel, it helps to sustain the political subtleties of participatory culture and what Burgess and Green call the "rich mundanity" of its conversations.[89] Political and social ideas often circulate online under the cover of idle chatter, such as memes, selfies, funny videos, comment chains, and reposts with new captions—a phenomenon that Melissa Harris-Lacewell, in a book on black public spaces that deserves to be updated for the age of Black Twitter, calls "the politics of everyday talk."[90] When, for example, I post an image of a woman in a hat with the caption, "When you have a nice hat," and a friend shares it with the caption, "When a guy at the party explains your dissertation to you"—how *insincere*, with this caption, the woman's smile looks!—the friend is telling an idle joke and also hooking the image into feminist discourse. When Tumblr users encourage each other to list their preferred pronouns in order to normalize the experiences of trans people, when 4channers mount a prank to associate the hand sign for OK with the white power movement, when a Twitter user calls attention to a post on We Rate Dogs that changed a dog's name to "George" from the Arabic "Kanan" and sets off a debate on white-washing, we encounter the lie in the conceit that wasting time online consists of empty discourse.[91] The President of the United States followed, for a short time, a cute-kitten account on Twitter called Emergency Kittens (apparently until someone told him that everyone could see which accounts he followed); had he continued to follow the account, how much time would have passed before the cute kittens took on, or were scrutinized for evidence of, political undertones?[92]

On a larger scale, the emerging canon of internet culture, like all canon formation, reflects a determination to create order out of a crisis of changing institutions. It has allowed people to set a pedestal under participatory culture and to celebrate its new values.[93] Consider Nyan Cat, the *japoniste* kitty that launched a thousand memes. After the image first appeared on the internet, viewers transformed it into a GIF, then into an animation with a Japanese electro-pop soundtrack. Others took it from there:

> Dozens of alternate animations and parodies were created. A bunch of musicians independently covered the song with piano, guitar, and Japanese lute. There's a dubstep remix.

There's a video of a guy on an exercise bike dressed up as Nyan Cat, pedaling to the music. There is a Nyan Cat flash video game. Between the image parodies, video mashups, audio remixes, games, and other references, the flying cat with the Pop Tart body is a memetic sensation with tens of thousands of iterations—and it's only been viral for a month, as of this writing.[94]

Some ten years later, I can report that Nyan Cat is still going strong. In 2011, as a "hack," students at the Massachusetts Institute of Technology mounted a giant artwork of Nyan Cat in the institute's main lobby.[95] The institute's administration reinstalled the hack in the main hallway of the humanities building, where it remains today. In the MIT Media Lab, the Center for Civic Media has adopted as an unofficial logo a picture of Nyan Cat in the style of the cover of an O'Reilly technology book, which Lorrie LeJeune, the center's assistant director and a former cover illustrator for O'Reilly, drew for a lark. The enshrinement of the meme at a major institution for technology research is meant to legitimize and celebrate certain values of participatory culture, such as whimsy, weirdness, the wisdom of crowds, the multiplication of authorship through memetic sharing, and transformative media engagement.

Can we connect the representative products of participatory culture with the technologies that sustain it, as scholars such as Alvin Kernan have done for print culture?[96] The cyberlaw scholar Jonathan Zittrain argues that we owe the extraordinary innovations of modern computer and networking technologies to their "generativity," or their openness to any new contribution, such as third-party software, that follows certain basic rules.[97] Burgess and Green build on his lead to argue for the value, in participatory culture, of "cultural generativity": the openness of platforms like YouTube to many uses, kinds of content, forms of play, which has resulted in a proliferation of content on those platforms.[98] So, too, we can identify generative online formats—and generative community cultures, as when a community builds higher-order levels of play atop a platform's ground rules by establishing tacit rules for the creation of good content. Like the rules of tic-tac-toe, which enable 255,168 potential games, or the rules of chess, which enable a number of potential games that exceeds the number of atoms in the universe, or the rules of the sonnet form, which have generated an unending library of sonnets, the combination of openness and constraint that governs memes has helped to make them a common currency online, enabling a tremendous number of possible moves. When, in 2010, the technology writer Clay Shirky called Lolcats "the stupidest possible creative act," he meant to praise the creative possibilities of even such a simple collaborative practice: the Lolcat format adheres to rules, which creates game-like conditions and therefore stimulating challenges, and the spread of Lolcats to every corner of the web demonstrates the productive potential of the spare time and energy of internet users (even if Lolcat creators, he thinks, aren't spending these well).[99]

Some time ago, when I opened a book about internet culture published in 2009, a foldout poster fell from the pages: a "family tree of internet cats."[100] In truth, the book didn't include much material on cats; the editors assumed that readers would get the joke, no explanation needed. The poster inspired the chapter that follows: on examining it, I realized that many of the internet cats we now know by name, and indeed the model of internet cat celebrity they represent, did not exist at the time of the family tree's creation. So I created a historical model (and, contra Clay Shirky, I believe *this* is the stupidest possible creative act to have arisen from the internet) of the Three Lives of Internet Cats.

The next chapter follows that timeline from the start of the web to the present day. The chapter draws substantially on the curator Jason Eppink's exhibition text for "How Cats Took over the Internet," a 2015 exhibition at the Museum of the Moving Image in New York City.

4 THE THREE LIVES OF INTERNET CATS

The history of internet cats can be divided into three periods: 1995–2004 (the webcam and personal blog era); 2005–2011 (the meme era); and 2011–present (the celebrity cat era).

1995–2004: WEBCAMS AND PERSONAL BLOGS

At the very end of the period 1995–2004, the earliest Web 2.0 platforms arrived on the web, as did meme culture in earnest. Catchphrases, jokes, practices like "the dozens," buzzworthy websites like Hampsterdance.com: all of these can be considered memes that predated Web 2.0 and, in some cases, the web. However, the self-aware internet culture of meme production and circulation arose in a later stage of the web's development. (The philosopher Ian Hacking's concept of *dynamic nominalism*, which contends that when we create new categories, we change our behavior in order to enact the meanings of those categories, suggests that we behave differently around catchphrases and their kin once we learn to call them *memes*. Classic meme templates did less to change internet culture than did the organizing concept of a meme.)[1]

At the beginning of this period, the web was, for many users, an unfamiliar place. We may find one index of this unfamiliarity in the omnipresent beige background of web videos from this period; not used to performing for faceless crowds online, people overwhelmingly chose the safety of anonymous blank walls.[2] But if performers found webcams unsettling, audiences found them fascinating. For a time, the most famous webcam on the internet was the Trojan Room Coffee Cam, which the Cambridge University Computer Laboratory brought online in 1991, and which showed a regularly updated image of the coffee pot in the lab's Trojan Room. Presumably its purpose was to let Cambridge researchers know when fresh coffee was ready, but it became famous because it seemed so random and arbitrary—because it assimilated so readily into the idea of the Weird Wide Web.[3]

For cat lovers, the biggest webcam on the internet was "KittyCam," which was devoted to watching the office cat, Kitty, of an advertising agency in California. The camera took a single stationary image every two minutes, and Kitty only appeared when she ambled in front of the stationary camera, but this was good enough for the public.[4] In 1998, KittyCam received over one million hits—big numbers for the time.[5] The webcam's administrators told journalists that they were surprised at the scale of the public's reaction: visitors often returned to the website to see updates several times daily, and some even visited town to see Kitty in person.[6] In a shrewd example of horizontal integration, the advertising agency, JointSolutions Marketing, developed KittyCam into a branch of the firm, selling Kitty merchandise and using Kitty to help promote the firm's move into digital ventures. The KittyCam website started to post "diary entries" written in the voice of Kitty. ("KITTY'S DIARY ... Thanksgiving is over, I had some turkey! Yummy! Now I'm looking forward to Christmas. Guess what? I just received my first Christmas gift! Thank you to Dave and Mel from England.") It also hosted a mailing list, a space where fans could exchange digital greeting cards, and an FAQ page that answered questions like "Why have a KittyCam?":

> Why not? Seriously, if people continue to visit KittyCam every day, is that not reason enough? On average, about two thousand people visit KittyCam every day. This makes her as popular as the average jazz band, novel, or public-access broadcast. More importantly, KittyCam has developed an online community of fans for whom it plays some part in their lives. Recently, we received a letter from a woman who spends most of her time caring for a bed-ridden husband. She called KittyCam her "window on the world" and appreciated the link it provided her to a cat thousands of miles away.[7]

In 1997, a couple in Massachusetts, Karen and Paul Watts, created a website called Pet of the Day, which, drawing from reader submissions, ran a photo and short feature every day about a pet (birds, cats, dogs, fish, snakes, and the rest), and which became one of the web's most popular animal sites.[8] In 1998, they siphoned off some of the content into a sister site, Cat of the Day.[9]

As images from this period show, early on, the iconography of internet animals differed from the iconography of internet animals today: less *cute*, less *weird*, less anthropomorphic—just dull, domestic pictures of household pets. Personal branding—the impulse to give one's pet a thematic "hook" (the cat is French, or grumpy, or easily startled, or impossibly fluffy), to use professional photography, to seek out visual elements that make images "pop"—is conspicuous by its absence.

Angry Cats

Given that snark and aggression have been defining postures on the internet since before the World Wide Web, it was inevitable that some websites about cats would absorb the snark, and that snarky websites about cats would capture the attention of the public. In 1998, a game designer named Cliff Bleszinski inaugurated a photography contest, called the Cat Scan Contest, in which people emailed him photographs of cats lying on scanners.[10] He hosted the entries on his personal website. "He's gotten more than 50 submissions," the *Wall Street Journal* reported just before the contest's original deadline. "They range from a surprised-looking little grey kitten to an unrecognizable clump of yellow-and-white fur that covers the entire viewing area. One contestant submitted an image of a large, plaid stuffed cat. Another would-be entry was prefaced by a question: 'My cat died three years ago and it's buried in the backyard. Do you take dead-cat scans?' Mr. Bleszinski does not."[11]

The contest caught the media's attention because its weirdness fit a familiar angle of news stories about the internet. The contest also had an obvious hook in its cruelty. Holding a cat on a live scanner risks harming the creature's eyes, "to say nothing of their psyches," said the *Post*, "after being sandwiched between a scanner's cover and bright lights." The possible danger to the cats gave the media a controversy to write about, and it didn't seem to dampen the pleasure that most people took in the pictures; it may indeed have sharpened the pleasure, following the Hollywood principle that cats in peril are funny.[12] Bleszinski posted new submissions for years after the original contest.

In 2000, a new website, bonsaikitten.com, became the object of widespread indignation, curiosity, and suspicion. The site provided instructions for trapping kittens inside glass containers and shaping them to fit their contours, thus creating living art objects. "Just as a topiary gardener produces bushes that take the forms of animals or any other thing," said the supposed author of the site, "Dr. Michael Wong Chang," "you no longer need be satisfied with a housepet having the same mundane shape as all other members of its species. With Bonsai Kitten, a world of variation awaits you, limited only by your own imagination."[13]

The site attracted worldwide news coverage, most of which noted that the site was a hoax.[14] The real author, a graduate student at MIT, reached out to news organizations to let them know that he had made up the idea of "bonsai kittens" and faked the pictures on the website. But word-of-mouth is a powerful force, and the site fueled visceral reactions with its gruesome accounts of body modification (bone shaping, feeding tubes, muscle relaxants) and pictures of kittens in jars. Pet lovers and animal rights groups, including the American Humane Society, sent angry letters and contacted politicians. The FBI served MIT with a subpoena requesting the site's subscriber information.[15]

Did the hoax have a point? Was it satire? The site's author told journalists that the answer was yes, but the message he described was inconsistent: the site satirized the devotion of cat lovers; the site satirized "the human belief of nature as a commodity."[16] One journalist, placing Bonsai Kittens in a common genre with the Cat Scan Contest, argued that the site simply aimed to provoke and that the provocation was the point, the in-joke that distinguished those who understood internet culture from the squares who didn't get it: "These websites proudly display the hate mail they receive. The asocial, pseudo-rebellious geek culture that inhabits so much of the internet thrives on notoriety. One person writes in Cat Scan's guestbook, 'Sick? Pretty much. Cruel? I think so. Wrong? Definitely. But mostly, you just have way too much time on your hands.' The internet is a vast playground for those with hours to squander and a predilection for taste-less humor."[17]

In 2000, a Microsoft employee named Alex Lebedeff, after sustaining injuries in an assault "with extreme preju-dice" from his pet cat, created a website called My Cat Hates You. The site, which gave captions with evil thoughts to pictures of Lebedeff's cats, quickly took off, as a colleague who helped manage the site noted on its "About" page: "I think it was within a week that alexal@ microsoft.com had become a miasma of evil cat images sent by an international audience; these were hundreds of people he did NOT know. Nor did he know how they found the site in the first place. But the internet being what it is, who could expect less?"[18]

The phrase "the internet being what it is" refers, not to the axiom that cats do well on the internet—this was not yet a memetic phenomenon in 2000—but rather to the axiom that people on the internet like to waste time and trade cruelties. My Cat Hates You was a cornucopia of petty cruelty; a review of the site's archive gallery shows cats of every description paired with captions that role-play villainy with obvious relish. ("Aleister hates you because you're an idiot. He can hospitalize you in one bite. He's done it before, and he can do it again." "This cat hates with such a hot hate, she can't even stand to be in the house when dorks come over. There are some loser-cooties that can't be licked off or hocked up in a hairball.")

Although this site predated cats' takeover of the web, it helped to pioneer the practice of repackaging a digital brand for print. By 2004, you could buy two books based on *My Cat Hates You*, as well as several kinds of calendars.[19] This kind of screen-to-page remediation has come to be the preferred path for the creators of viral web phenomena. Jonny Sun has a book; Humans of New York has a book; Awkward Family Photos has a book; We Rate Dogs has two books; Lolcats have multiple books. A book in print is still a powerful sign of arrival for the flagbearers of new media.

Other cat ephemera on the internet during these years: in 2002, Rathergood.com, a weird-news aggregator blog in the vein of Fark and Something Awful, released a Flash animation in which kittens rocked out to Top 40 music, which became a hit. In 2003, internet users started circulating pictures of their cats with objects balanced on their bodies; one commenter described the fad as "Cat Buckaroo," or "the magical art of placing various objects on a sleeping cat and seeing who can get the most on before the cat wakes up in a disgruntled mood and slouches off." In time, the fad spawned websites like Stuff on My Cat (2005) and Cat Stackers (2010).[20]

The Infinite Cat Project

If you take interest in the history of hardware, I suggest you check out the Infinite Cat Project. In 2003, a participant on an Apple web forum took a picture of his cat (named Frankie) examining a picture of himself on a computer screen. He made the image still more recursive by putting the new picture on his computer screen, getting his cat to look at it, then taking another picture. He uploaded the result to the forum, and the concept took off: forum users took pictures of their cats looking at new iterations of the image on their home computers. They helpfully labeled new images with the names of the featured cats, so that you knew, a few turns in, that you were looking at an image of Tiger watching Farrusko watching Skinny White Boy watching Peaker watching Brit watching Plien watching Eunheui watching Datsa watching Tasha watching Duma watching 99 watching Snowball watching Hawkeye watching Copper watching Fritz watching Zoot watching Abby watching Frankie watching Poozy watching Frankie watching Sammy watching Frankie.[21] Finally a web designer named Mike Stanfill created a website to host the project in perpetuity, which he called the Infinite Cat Project.[22]

As of this writing, the website records 1,823 photos of cats looking at cats. As Jason Eppink notes, the website is also an exhibition of the changes in home computer technology that have taken place since 2004. As you move back through the timeline of cats, you see slender notebooks transform into enormous boxes. (Stanhope wrote a post in 2004 that acknowledged that many computer users did not own digital cameras. He advised, "Just use a normal, film-type camera and when you get your film developed have it saved to a CD, a very inexpensive process nowadays. Then choose the best picture off the disc and email a copy to me.")[23]

Frank the Cat

A final cat tale can help to round out this period: that of Frank the Cat, who has a claim to the title of first celebrity cat on the English-speaking internet. In January 2002, a tabby named Frank was hit by a car in Cambridge, England. Good Samaritans found the injured cat and brought him to a veterinary hospital, where vets repaired his broken pelvis. Frank's owner wanted to thank the cat's anonymous rescuers, so he set up a webcam (at the address cathospital.co.uk) that showed a continuous video of Frank's recovery, on the chance that the site would attract their attention.[24]

Frank became an unexpected viral celebrity. Within a few weeks of the site going up, more than 500,000 people had seen it; by the middle of May, some 12,000 unique visitors logged in every day. By the year's end, the site had more than four and a half million visitors.[25] "The response has been overwhelming," Frank's owner told a journalist. "But everyone loves a cuddly animal and the fact he is defenseless and injured probably adds to his appeal."[26] Yahoo selected the site as one of the top websites of 2002. Letters and get-well cards poured in.

The Good Samaritans got in touch with Frank's owner. I preserve their names here: Alex Whan and David Hawes.[27]

2005–2011: THE MEME ERA

The *New York Times* was an early print outlet to recognize the power of cats as a symbol on the web. In 2005, an article titled "Internet's Best Friend (Let Me Count the Ways)" proclaimed the cat to be the web's favorite animal: "On the Web you'll find the Infinite Cat Project but no Infinite Dog. My Cat Hates You is big on the Web, but there is no site named My Dog Hates You. . . . Cats are the Web's it-animals. They're everywhere."

Ultimately, the article argued that cats, surly and solitary as they are, resemble internet users—and that we find mystery and fascination in the inner lives of cats, whereas the inner lives of dogs are not nearly so mysterious.[28] Whether netizens are truly catlike is unprovable—the argument of this book is that their affiliation with cats is cultural, not natural—but it is true that people want to scrutinize the inner lives of cats more than they do dogs. I once asked Mary Salvig, a curator at the Archives of American Art who combed mountains of archival materials to prepare an exhibition of artists' paintings, drawings, and photographs of their cats, whether artists tend, in correspondence, to treat their dogs differently from their cats. Yes, she said: "Cats are the subject of a lot more thought for artists. They expend a lot of space telling stories and writing about their cats. They want to explain what they think the cat is thinking."[29]

Yet the *Times* article does not mention the indelicate spaces, like 4chan, Something Awful, Fark, and Rathergood, that provided the sources of the web's new fascination with cat content.[30] These sites created the members of the "family tree of internet cats" that fell out of my library book. This is to say they created *memes*: reproducible, reconfigurable, made for a repetitive remix economy that operates by circulating shifting repetitions of the same thing.

From the perspective of the 2020s, what is notable about the famous cats of the meme era is they don't have names. There is no Maru, no Grumpy Cat, no Lil Bub, no Venus, no Zelda. Instead, they have labels, like Happycat and Long Cat, and each cat exists as a single image.

Thus (and here I refer to the family tree of internet cats) Happycat begat Lord Happycat, who begat Pope Happycat I, who begat Holy Kitty. And Happycat begat Ceiling Cat, who begat Medieval Ceiling Cat, who begat Emperor Cat and Bodybuilder Cat. And the sons of Emperor Cat were Egypt Cats, Tubcat, and Star Wars Cats, who begat Robot Cat. And Happycat begat Drill Cat, who begat Popcorn Cat, who begat Limecat and Scared Kitty. Forsooth the sons of Limecat were Lemoncat and Orangecat. The sons of Lemoncat were Moon Cat and Fish Bowl Cat. And the son of Orangecat was Fat Cat, who begat Fire Cat, Lovely Kitty, Tankcat, Corncat, and Tilt Wet Kitty. And Tankcat begat Breadcat; and Breadcat began to be mighty in the earth. Tilt Wet Kitty begat Guess Who Cat, who begat Longcat, and Longcat of Love, and Monorail Cat. And Longcat begat Looooooooongcat, and to Looooooooongcat was born two sons: King Pimp Cat and Scanned Cat. Fire Cat begat Wig Cat and Devil Cat, who begat Tacgnol, who begat Tactrohs and Internet Cat, who begat Tech Support Cat, who begat Invisible Bike Cat and Evil Cat, who begat Crazy Eyed Cat, Hissy JelliBelli, and Smiley Cat, who begat Patriotic Cat and Pirat Cat, who begat Screamin' Steven and Goodbye Kitty, who begat Amused Cat. And I have only referred, by this point, to a small portion of the cats in the family tree's branches.

I doubt this tree is a perfect record of generational descent. (Why wouldn't Tacgnol, which is Longcat backwards, descend from Longcat?) But it doesn't mean to be accurate. It means to playfully reinforce the association between cats and the internet and also to emphasize, through the structure of a family tree, the iterative, expansive character of the meme economy. We like the classics, but we also need novelties to show that we're au courant. Only an insider knows Invisible Bike Cat when the meme is fresh, and only an insider knows when Invisible Bike Cat is over.

At around the same time that Lolcats became a hit on 4chan and Something Awful, a meme called Advice Dog began to circulate on these sites: an image macro of a Golden Retriever with a ditzy look, with captions that deliver conspicuously poor advice. ("WALK ON RED. PEOPLE CAN'T SEE YOU.") Advice Dog inaugurated a long chain of animal memes: Business Cat ("CANCEL MY 3 O'CLOCK. I NEED TO WATCH THIS BIRD"), Anxiety Cat ("HAVE TO EMAIL A DOCUMENT. CHECK 12 TIMES THAT IT'S THE RIGHT FILE"), and Courage Wolf ("WHAT DOESN'T KILL YOU IS GOING TO DIE").[31] Advice Animals appeal to the desire to explain what an animal is thinking, though the explanation, in this case, is simply that the animal thinks what we think. When artists in earlier days sent pictures of their pets in their letters, Salvig says, the pets were meant, in part, to represent an aspect of the artist. The animals of Advice Animals channel us in a more obvious way. Additionally, animal memes take the quintessential internet genre of the alienated animal past the classic Lolcat model, in part as a way of asserting knowledge of internet culture. *I'm so sophisticated that I don't have to use a cat meme; I can use a sloth meme instead.*

Cat Videos

2005 was the year that YouTube came to the internet. As it happens, the platform's creators, Steve Chen and Chad Hurley, demonstrated the platform's potential to investors by showing a test video of Chen's cat hunting yarn. (They got funding, and in December the platform went public. Less than a year afterward, Google bought the platform for some $1.65 billion.)[32] A 2018 book by Kevin Allocca, the Head of Culture and Trends at YouTube, measures the virality of YouTube videos—Rebecca Black's "Friday," for instance—by comparing them with the "aggregate of cat video viewership." He never explains why he uses cat videos as his yardstick for virality. He doesn't need to; he understands that readers will get the joke.[33]

Chen and Hurley expected that people would use YouTube mainly to share home videos, which is why the test videos they used for the platform were mundane slices of life: a cat batting at yarn, a trip to the zoo. As it happened, people had bigger ideas for the site. They choreographed elaborate dances and lip-synching routines; they overlaid normal videos with dramatic music and effects; they created animated sketches; they launched serialized, increasingly professional-looking video diaries; they shared bootleg clips from television. They also shared cat videos, but the biggest performers in this category often had the same semiprofessional touch. The earliest cats to go viral on YouTube—Maru, a Japanese cat who does adorable things with boxes; "Surprise Kitten," a kitten who responds to tickling with human gestures of delight; "Keyboard Cat," a cat who seems to play an electronic keyboard; "Henri, le Chat Noir," a series in which a cat broods while a voiceover drops surly aperçus in a French accent—were not caught in ordinary moments, but rather had gimmicks, dramatic overlays, professional-level videography, or special effects.[34]

In 2012, the Walker Art Center in Minneapolis inaugurated a tradition called the Internet Cat Video Festival, an annual daylong event in which crowds gathered to watch a selection of internet cat videos on a huge outdoor screen, and to see the Walker Center give a "Golden Kitty Award" to a video creator of the public's choice. The winner was Will Braden, the creator of "Henri, le Chat Noir." He received, as a trophy, a maneki-neko figurine with the kanji character for "Fortune" on its belly.[35]

Braden later told a documentary team, "It's hard for me to think about the Henri videos as, like, super high art. I mean, they're meant to just be silly, and to a certain extent, just to be a parody. And they're a different kind of cat video. But at the same time, if people weren't so into cat videos, then no one would be interested in 'Henri.' If I had made 'Henri' with a bunny, no one would have cared."[36]

2012–PRESENT: CELEBRITY CATS

Since around 2012, celebrity cats have defined what one writer calls "the online cat-industrial complex."[37] The most famous internet cats to emerge in recent years have names: Colonel Meow, Garfi, Grumpy Cat, Hamilton the Hipster Cat, Lil Bub, Mao, Maru, Nala, Princess Monster Truck, Pudge, Remy, Rolf, Sam Has Eyebrows, Shironeko, Snoopybabe, Venus, Waffles, and Zelda, among many, many others. The YouTube Partner Program, which helps content creators to monetize their channels, distinguishes between comedy partners, music partners, and "cat partners," among others. Reportedly, YouTube has over a hundred cat partners in Japan alone.[38] More and more cat owners are creating YouTube, Twitter, and Instagram accounts for their pets, hoping to win fame and fortune through follows, likes, and shares. The most famous cats are worth fortunes; many of them have the same manager, Ben Lashes, who negotiates advertising, merchandise, and media tie-ins on behalf of his feline clients.[39]

In a certain respect, the rise of celebrity cats answers a question about internet economics that economists and media theorists have been debating for decades. That question is whether the internet will flatten the playing field so that a few superstars no longer reap most of the consumer demand in a given area. Chris Anderson, the editor-in-chief of *Wired* magazine, gave this idea its most famous articulation in his 2006 book, *The Long Tail: Why the Future of Business Is Selling Less of More.*[40] There, Anderson argues that the web's new content production and distribution channels will enable consumers to buy narrower niches of products, less popular but more to their individual tastes. (The narrowing demand for niches constitutes the *long tail.*) Netflix, Apple's iTunes, and YouTube represent long-tail businesses in the sense that they allow users to find and purchase items that aren't nearly popular enough to appear in brick-and-mortar stores.[41] As the web matures, he argued, many markets that now operate according to the principles of what economists call a *blockbuster economy* will switch to economies governed by the long tail.

More recently, Anita Elberse, a professor at Harvard Business School, has shown that the rise of new content production and distribution channels on the web does not mean that old rules cease to apply. Data show that consumers have not changed their behavior online: "As demand shifts from offline retailers with limited shelf space to online channels with much larger assortments, the sales distribution is not getting fatter in the tail. On the contrary, as time goes on and consumers buy more goods online, the tail is getting longer but decidedly thinner."[42] In fact, in the digital marketplace, blockbusters are more important than ever: although the long tail is lengthening, in the sense that unpopular items are finding buyers, blockbusters are gaining a larger proportion of total sales. The reasons for this are, first, that casual buyers prefer blockbusters, which they feel they can trust; and second, that even while using the borderless, anonymous internet, we still rely on recommendations from friends. Popularity begets popularity.[43]

We might therefore view the rise of celebrity cats as an inevitable extension of the maturing of the web as a marketplace. The Pareto Principle suggests that 20 percent of the cats online should get 80 percent of the attention; and while the work of checking this projection must be left to a heroic quantitative analyst at some future date, we can at least say that the social media channels of superstars like Grumpy Cat and Lil Bub have subscriber counts that vastly dwarf those of channels belonging to the large number of would-be celebrity cats out there. To give a sense of the internet cat landscape in the year 2020, I will mention a few of the web's celebrity cats here.

Maru and the Musashis

By the numbers, Maru is the most famous cat on the internet. In 2016, he won a Guinness World Record for the number of times that videos of a single animal had been viewed on YouTube—more than 325 million at that date. Born in 2007, Maru is a Scottish Fold cat—soft, chubby, and fond of sitting in boxes. Maru is a champion at sitting in boxes: he dives into deep boxes, he lounges in long boxes, he squeezes into teeny boxes.[44] Although Maru doesn't make public appearances, he has starred on Japanese commercials, and you can buy an array of Maru-branded calendars and books.[45]

A writer for *Wired* magazine, Gideon Lewis-Kraus, attempted to meet Maru in 2012. Ultimately, he had to write what journalists call a "write-around"—a profile in which the writer never meets the subject—because Maru is closely guarded and shrouded in secrecy; even her owner's location is unknown. "Maru's supervisory documentarian is named Mugumogu, but beyond that fact, hardly anything is known about her," he wrote:

> When I write Maru's US book publicist—you read that right—it turns out that she knows no more than you or I. The publicist loops in Maru's US book editor, who offers to pass along some interview questions to Mugumogu's Japanese agent, who could have them translated, answered, and sent back. . . . A few days later the publicist writes back: Impossible. I'm welcome to write to the Japanese agent, she says, but I should know that not even the agent knows who Mugumogu is; her correspondence all goes through Maru's Japanese publisher. . . . I commence months of fruitlessly obsequious email courtship with Mugumogu but ultimately to no avail.[46]

Though he could not get in touch with Maru, he did talk with another group of internet-famous cats, the Musashis.

The Musashis are a "cat band," and they are just one of many cat bands on the internet. In 2007, their owner, a sound engineer and musician, used audio clips of his five cats meowing to create a cover of "Jingle Bells," which he put on YouTube to advertise his professional skills. YouTube Japan featured the video on its homepage; then YouTube featured the video on its global homepage. Before long, the video had more than a million hits.[47] The Musashis made a deal with a company called Stardust Promotion to produce music and video content: the Musashis meowing "Auld Lang Syne" for mobile phones, the Musashis meowing with pop stars, the Musashis meowing the theme song for a network TV drama.[48] The Musashis also got a book deal. Naturally.

Lil Bub

In 2011, Mike Bridavsky uploaded photographs of his new kitten, Lil Bub, to Tumblr. He had rescued the kitten from a feral colony earlier that year, as she clearly had special needs. (Bub's jaw was underdeveloped and she lacked teeth, which meant that her tongue perpetually stuck out. Her eyes were unusually large for a cat. Lil Bub passed away in 2019, but for most of her life, her health was reportedly good.) The photos quickly migrated to Reddit and from there to Buzzfeed.[49] By 2012, Lil Bub was the subject of adoring journalistic coverage.[50] Today, at a brick-and-mortar store in her hometown of Bloomington, Indiana, you can buy Lil Bub mugs, postcards, tote bags, T-shirts, and stickers, among other merchandise—which is also available on the web. She starred, from 2013 to 2014, in "Lil Bub's Big Show," a web series with high production values in which Bub "interviewed" celebrity guests. She headlined in the documentary Lil Bub & Friendz, which premiered at the Tribeca Film Festival in 2013; the film won the Tribeca Online Festival Best Feature Film. And, of course, she had a book.[51]

"She's the most photogenic cat in the world," Bridavisky, who seems like a chill guy, says in *Lil Bub & Friendz*. "So I take a picture, and I put it on Tumblr. And people started responding to it. It's like, whoa, and then people I don't know are sending me messages. One is that she looks so different, but is still cute. So it's, like, challenging what the standard is for cuteness, or, you know, it's okay to be different and still be appreciated. And then, out of nowhere, suddenly all this awesome stuff started happening."[52]

The documentary, like Lil Bub's web series, makes the surprising choice to present Lil Bub in the frame of science fiction. ("Deep within the far reaches of the universe, in a galaxy not yet known to us humans, lived a tiny and complex creature, Lil Bub. One day, Bub decided to leave her planet and venture off into the darkness of space. This is her story.") This origin story plays on her alien looks and the ease she has with travel, Bridavisky says.[53] It also sets genre expectations for her audience; her fictional frame is like that of the title character of the novel *The Little Prince* (1943), which is to say that it's science fiction but also a fairy tale. Lil Bub's success—that is, the amount of love she found in the world—plays, in this frame, as the fairy-tale device that J.R.R. Tolkien called *eucatastrophe*: for a disabled feral kitten, life should be brutal and short, but against all odds, it isn't. The devotion and imagination of her owner helped to make her such an appealing character, though he treated his share of his cat's fame with wry skepticism.

"I don't understand how Mike hasn't found love from this yet," one of Bridavisky's friends says in *Lil Bub & Friendz*. "All these girls are commenting on Gawker about you, how hot you are. I know u don't like to be in the spotlight here, but it is true."

"I dated this girl for a short period of time," Bridavisky replies. "And she's like, 'I told my mom about you. I told her that you own a recording studio and you have a famous cat.' And her mom said, 'Yeah, not that guy.'"[54]

Grumpy Cat

In 2012, a young man named Bryan Bundensen posted to Reddit a picture of a cat named Tardar Sauce, whose markings gave her a permanently grumpy look. The post was titled, "Meet Grumpy Cat." Responses flooded in: "Why are you so grumpy cat you don't even pay taxes, get a fucking job." "I want a subreddit of just grumpy cats." Someone posted an image macro of the cat's face with the caption, "I HAD FUN ONCE / IT WAS AWFUL." (The joke was taken from a comic by the Canadian artist Kate Beaton.)[55] A commenter later replied in the thread, "I bet you didn't know how viral this cat would be in 5 months."[56]

The cat's image rose quickly to the top of a subreddit called Advice Animals, which curates images in the Advice Animals genre that 4chan created. It spread rapidly to other parts of the internet, while Bundensen (the brother of Tardar Sauce's owner, Tabatha Bundensen) fanned the flames by posting new images to Reddit: "Good morning from Grumpy Cat!" "The Daily Grump | October 11." "Grumpy Cat and Pokey." "Tard the Grumpy Cat Returns." Finally, the cat reached such a level of virality that the siblings presumably realized that they had a brand. The cat's photos were deleted from Imgur (a photo-hosting site associated with Reddit) and started to be hosted on www.grumpycats.com.

Like Lil Bub, Grumpy Cat (the cat's stage name) had visible disabilities but good health. She had feline dwarfism, which, combined with an underbite and fortuitous coloring, gave her the permanent appearance of a scowl. Her appeal to internet users was concrete and immediate. When her owner held a question-and-answer session on Reddit, a commenter wrote:

> This isn't a question and I feel like it's kind of a weird thing to say, but I want you to know how much Grumpy Cat means to me. I just started working two full time jobs and I'm generally tired and cranky all the time. My fiance knows that when I'm in a mood (which is often these days) referencing grumpy cat will always make me smile. Sometimes

he texts me pictures of grumpy cat throughout the day when I'm at work. Also when I'm being particularly unpleasant, he calls me 'grumpy cat' which, again, always kind of makes me smile.

Another commenter wrote, "First comment ever/delurking to proclaim my love for this cat. I don't even like cats. I'm allergic to cats. But Grumpy Cat appeals to my soul."[57]

As Grumpy Cat's fame grew, her owner began selling merchandise and got her a monetized YouTube channel. The cat's scowl adorned baby bibs, calendars, car decals, coffee mugs, keychains, pillows, office supplies, pajamas, plush animals, slippers, shirts, and socks, among other merchandise. She was the face of Friskies.[58] She had her own brand of "coffee drink."[59] In 2014, she got a movie, *Grumpy Cat's Worst Christmas Ever*.[60] (In an instance of perfect casting, Aubrey Plaza provides Grumpy Cat's voice.)

These days, internet fame looks the same as regular fame, as Ben Lashes remarked to a filmmaker when talking about a trip that Grumpy Cat made to New York City:

People on the streets of New York were swarming around everywhere that we went because we had to walk from place to place. We had some people that would walk by and then just freeze and be like, 'Oh my gosh, is that—is that Grumpy Cat? No effin' way!'[61] And one girl walking up, she's like, 'Oh my gosh, is it really Grumpy Cat?' She started hyperventilating and jumping up and down. She had tears in her eyes. It was like John Lennon was right there back to life. It was totally insane. Grumpy Cat is totally the next big cat."[62]

Grumpy Cat passed away in May 2019. She was publicly mourned the world over.

Curious Zelda

What is it like to be the owner of a famous cat? Recently, I interviewed Matt Taghioff, the owner of a cat named Zelda who has (at the time of this writing) more than 190,000 followers on Twitter.[63] Taghioff, then a 32-year-old customer service manager living in Beckenham, Kent, was eager to stress that Zelda is not, so to speak, what he does for a living. "I'm not framing Zelda as my work and enterprise," he said. "It's an incredibly pure account. It was bred out of being a side hobby."

"There are plans to write a book," he added—publishers and literary agents had been reaching out to him.

Zelda is a cat whose eyes, which bug out a little, seem to wear a perpetual expression of surprise. She has black-and-white markings that accentuate the expression. From some angles, she resembles an ink painting of a frog from the Edo period; from others, she resembles Beaker from the Muppets. Like many cat accounts on Twitter, Zelda's account (@CuriousZelda) uses the first person in the captions that accompany the images; but unlike many such accounts, Zelda's does not use baby talk or lolspeak. Instead, the captions offer explanations for why she looks surprised ("RUN FOR YOUR LIVES. SOMETHING ORDINARY IS ABOUT TO HAPPEN"; "Suddenly, it dawned on me that I had been naked my whole life").[64] Or "she" describes the havoc she is about to wreak upon her home, which you are free to imagine is also your home ("There's no such thing as scratch resistant"; "Today, I will mostly be reducing the value of our home").[65] Or she takes flights of whimsy, imagining that she has been folded like laundry ("Always leave your Zelda in the folded position") or that her pupils are huge because they signal a fully charged battery ("Please be careful not to overcharge your Zelda").[66]

Sometimes she expresses her thoughts as poetry:

See a housefly
So discreet
Tiny war cry
Then I eat[67]

I thought I saw my nemesis
I sensed he was around
In truth I had imagined it
And yet I stood my ground[68]

Scratch the sofa
Claw the bed
Tear the curtain
Still get fed[69]

Zelda's subscribers are a doting and enthusiastic community. They send pictures of their own cats. They offer new explanations for why Zelda looks surprised. They create Zelda fan art.[70] Taghioff has even received proposals of marriage from strangers on Twitter.[71]

Taghioff adopted Zelda from a rescue shelter in 2014. "I went to a charity, the Mayhew rescue shelter, to look for a black cat," he said. "Zelda was the one and only cat I met that day. After a short but intense staring match, she came over to me and was incredibly loving."

The shelter had feared that her bug-eyed look would scare off potential adopters. The online adoption ad for the tuxedo cat read, "Don't be put off by my spooked expression." As she became accustomed to living in a flat with a human roommate, she grew less skittish and more confident; but her expression never changed.

"When friends visited, her expressions were always a talking point," he said. "There's so much going on in her eyes, and you can come up with so many reasons or things for her to be startled about. I had a lot of friends and colleagues at work who encouraged me to put her face on the internet." He registered a Twitter account for Zelda in 2015 and started tweeting in early 2016.

Our impulse to project narratives onto her helps to account for her appeal, he suggested: "Cats have this remarkable way of drawing our attention and getting us to make way for them in some way, make allowances for them. They have a sense of entitlement as they sprawl across the doorway. Dogs have an immediate availability that seems easier to read."

On Twitter, he started his project with the goal of making her seem as alive on the screen as he could. He learned a few tricks from studying other internet cats. "One of the things I always thought while looking at cats and memes online is: *I wish I had this cat in my life*," he said. "I make believe that she's not just appearing on Twitter, she's in their homes. Trashing their homes, zooming around their living rooms, sleeping on their stairs. People welcome that, because they want Zelda in their lives."

As for his choice not to use baby talk, "It's kind of been a conscious decision and having a feel to it," he said. "Early when Zelda was on Twitter, she misspelled some words. I think she has learned from interacting with her audience. She's still impulsive, as revealed in her questionable behaviors. But she has a lot of time on her paws to think. So it doesn't make sense to me that she would use babyish language."

Zelda's audience also contributed pieces to her backstory, he said: "For instance, that she drinks a lot of coffee, and that she's a creature that can see through time and see the end of the world." (Having spent time looking through Zelda fan art and postings, I can report that the Zelda lore is deep.)

Zelda's subscriber count rose slowly, then quickly. Now and then, the count would get a boost when someone posted pictures of Zelda to Imgur or Reddit. In 2017, as she passed 24,000 followers, journalists began to write stories about the account. One day, his uncle texted him to share the news that "Curious Zelda" was a quiz selection on a radio quiz show on BBC2. Book publishers started to reach out to him: "They see from Twitter that there's a good opportunity to transfer to a book," he said. (The book *The Adventures of a Curious Cat: Wit and Wisdom from Curious Zelda, Purr-fect for Cats and their Humans* came out from Sphere Books in 2019.)

At the time that I spoke to him, that's where he was: weighing his options and figuring out what direction to take. The book would happen, he said, but he hoped to maintain the account's purity. "Twitter doesn't have a natural way of monetizing," he said. "I started the account because I saw something fun to do. Not to advertise products and do partnerships. She really has her own kind of personality. She doesn't just quote and promote for the sake of it. She's clearly a very thoughtful kitty."

THE PURR-AMID OF SUCCESS

In a 2000 article, the literary critic Franco Moretti argued that literary genres ultimately arise, not from writers or from cultural arbiters, but from audiences.[72] Moretti begins by citing a model, by the economists Arthur De Vany and W. David Walls, of the blockbuster economy of the movie industry. As De Vany and Walls note, the movie industry is carried by its hits, with 80 percent of the box office going to 20 percent of the movies in theaters. The problem is that nobody can reliably predict what makes a hit. Filmgoers produce hits by recommending films they like to others, creating an "information cascade" of recommendations begetting recommendations; but the fact that filmgoers *like* a film is sometimes a surprise to everyone involved. ("Film audiences make hits or flops and they do it, not by revealing preferences they already have, but by discovering what they like," De Vany and Walls write. "When they see a movie they like, they make a discovery and they tell their friends about it; reviewers do this too. This information is transmitted to other consumers and demand develops dynamically over time as the audience sequentially discovers and reveals its demand.")[73]

Moretti argues that the literary marketplace works the same way. But literary scholars may be able to explain, in the case of the literary marketplace, what economists are not obliged to explain about the film marketplace: namely, which formal devices appealed to a given audience at a given time, inspiring the information cascade. In the case of detective stories, for instance, literary scholars may note that most detective stories published in the day of Sir Arthur Conan Doyle did not have the features of what is now the "classic" detective story: material clues, visible to though unnoticed by the reader, that lead the detective to his conclusion. Even Doyle's Sherlock Holmes stories did not always have these features. But many of them did; and readers liked and recommended Doyle's stories over the stories of his rivals in the detective genre, until finally Sherlock Holmes was the figure of the fictional detective par excellence.[74]

Observers of our own time have already begun to make guesses, and good ones, about what formal features the people of the internet like in celebrity cats. They like cuteness, which cats with babyish features and unusually large eyes have to a special degree. They like vulnerability, which they can easily read into the visible disabilities of Lil Bub and Grumpy Cat or, for that matter, the startled look of Zelda. They like what the poet John Keats called *negative capability*: Grumpy Cat inspires us to supply endless explanations as to *why* she is grumpy, never giving us the shallow satisfaction of a definite answer. And they like, it seems, an element of weirdness. Bub flies around in a spaceship; Zelda can see the end of the world; the cats of Black Metal Cats expose the eerie lurking in the everyday. Listening to the music of the Musashis, Lewis-Kraus says he finds something appealing in its alien quality, which "is hard not to read as the kind of netherworldly incursion that used to get cats set ritualistically on fire."[75]

EPILOGUE

Late Adopter

When I started work on this book, I was Not a Cat Person. But I try to be thorough, so once research was underway, I reached out to a shelter in Brooklyn and asked to foster a kitten.

The shelter chose a small black kitten. I put him in my apartment's bathroom, at first, so that he couldn't hide where I couldn't find him. When I started to pet him, an immense purr rose and filled the little room, vibrating off the walls. I felt like I was using echolocation. *Aaron Purr,* I thought, and that was that.

"You know what the problem is?" My father asked that day by phone.

"What?" I asked.

"You're going to keep the cat."

"I'm not," I said, and explained why for the next ten minutes.

As the days passed, I posted updates on Facebook:

Dog and kitten are curled up together.

Now Victor is imitating the cat. Cat does something, Victor tries to do it.

More imitation: cat grooms cat; Victor tries to groom cat.

Dog and cat are cuddled up again. I don't want to breathlessly live-blog this relationship, but here we are.

Kitten's favorite place to nap is on the desk by my computer. I guess this is okay for the time being.

The cat has earned my respect. But that doesn't mean my loyalties have changed.

Finally, I told my father on the phone, "I'm going to keep the cat."

"Surprise, surprise," he said.

Aaron Purr will never be a Twitter star or an Instagram glamour-puss. He hates having his picture taken and stalks away if I bring a camera near him. If I may project human traits onto him, he is deliberate, reserved, and thoughtful.

It's humbling to like a cat after spending so much energy complaining about them. I'll go further and say, since Victor can't read, that I'm probably a cat person. I foster kittens regularly these days, and they are very much present as characters in the home: goofy, gentlemanly, shy, sly, imperious; amusing companions during solitary work. I've learned more about how to read feline body language, and it turns out that cats are full of emotion.

Having been reminded so pointedly that I can't predict the turns in my own life, I should refrain, I think, from pretending that I can say much about the future of the internet. Yet we can likely be confident that whatever turns the internet takes, the tubes will remain cat-shaped: frivolous, subversive, cute, mean, and weird, with communities of users fighting endless battles over the imaginary heart of the web, and with play and politics in perpetual mutual reinforcement.

ACKNOWLEDGMENTS

This book could not exist without the support of brilliant friends, sources, and colleagues. D. E. Wittkower, a central node in the internet--cat scholarly community, provided indispensable resources and advice. Jason Eppink, the curator of Digital Media at the Museum of the Moving Image, shared exhibition files that substantially informed Chapter 5 and gave insightful comments on the manuscript. Ethan Zuckerman and Nate Matias, incisive scholars of the networked world, shared their time and expertise to talk about cats, the internet, and internet cats. I am also grateful to Matt Taghioff, the personal assistant of Curious Zelda, for his insights into the world of internet fame.

Portions of this book previously appeared in _Public Books_ and _New Media & Society_. I am grateful to their editors, Sharon Marcus, Caitlin Zaloom, and Steve Jones, for their guidance and editorial expertise.

Kate Wahl, editor-in-chief of Stanford University Press, has guided this project from the beginning. To her, and to the anonymous readers for the press, I owe a great debt.

NOTES

INTRODUCTION

1. Dana Perino, *Let Me Tell You about Jasper* (a Fox News host discusses dogs) (New York: Twelve, 2016); Mary Oliver, *Dog Songs* (poems and an essay on dogs) (New York: Penguin, 2013); Mike Ritland, *Trident K9 Warriors* (combat dogs) (New York: St. Martin's, 2015); Seth Casteel, *Underwater Dogs* ("photographs of dogs under water") (New York: Little, Brown and Company, 2012); Maria Goodavage, *Soldier Dogs* (combat dogs) (New York: Dutton, 2012); Jim Gorant, *The Lost Dogs* (dogs saved from a dogfighting ring) (New York: Avery, 2011); Malcolm Gladwell, *What the Dog Saw* (Gladwellian essays; the title essay focuses on a dog trainer) (New York: Penguin, 2015); Alexandra Horowitz, *Inside of a Dog* (dog psychology) (New York: Scribner, 2010); Dean Koontz, *A Big Little Life* (adopting a dog) (New York: Random House, 2011); Mark R. Levin, *Rescuing Sprite* (adopting a dog) (New York: Threshold, 2009); Anna Quindlen, *Good Dog. Stay* (raising a dog) (New York: Random House, 2007); Ted Kerasote, *Merle's Door* (adopting a dog) (New York: Mariner Books, 2008); Jon Katz, *Dog Days* (raising dogs) (New York: Villard, 2007); John Grogan, *Marley*

and Me (raising a dog) (New York: William Morrow, 2005); John O'Hurley, *It's Okay to Miss the Bed on the First Jump* (living with dogs) (New York: Hudson Street, 2006).

2. Gwen Cooper, *Homer's Odyssey* (adopting a blind cat) (Delacorte, 2010).

3. On the collision of stardom with the internet, see, for example, Rex Sorgatz, "The Microfame Game," *New York*, June 17, 2008, http://nymag.com/news/media/47958/; and Chris Anderson, *The Long Tail: Why the Future of Business Is Selling Less of More* (New York: Hyperion, 2006).

4. Caitlin Dewey, "Meet the Internet's Earliest Cat Lovers—and the Trolls Who Terrorized Them," *Washington Post*, August 8, 2014, https://www.washingtonpost.com/news/the-intersect/wp/2014/08/08/meet-the-internets-earliest-cat-lovers-and-the-trolls-who-terrorized-them/.

5. Kenneth Goldsmith, *Wasting Time on the Internet* (New York: HarperCollins, 2016).

6. The 2018 book *Disrupting the Digital Humanities* has a similar design: a snarling cat on the cover, with no mention of cats, nor any mention needed, inside the book's pages. Dorothy Kim and Jesse Stommel, eds., *Disrupting the Digital Humanities* (New York: Punctum, 2018).

7. Anonymous, "Asian Leaders Are in the Vanguard of Social Media," *The Economist*, February 8, 2018, https://www.economist.com/asia/2018/02/08/asian-leaders-are-in-the-vanguard-of-social-media; Kevin Roose, "Online Cesspool Got You Down? You Can Clean It Up, for a Price," *New York Times Magazine*, November 13, 2019, https://www.nytimes.com/interactive/2019/11/13/magazine/internet-premium.html; "So the Internet Didn't Turn Out the Way We Hoped. Where Do We Go from Here?," *New York Times Magazine*, November 14, 2019, https://www.nytimes.com/interactive/2019/11/14/magazine/internet-future-dream.html.

8. Ben Smith, "11 BuzzFeed Lists that Explain the World," *Foreign Policy* no. 200, May-June 2013, 20–21, https://foreignpolicy.com/2013/04/29/11-buzzfeed-lists-that-explain-the-world/.

9. Caitlin McGarry, "Reddit's Grand Vision: Come for the Cats, Stay for the Empathy," *PC World*, March 10, 2017, https://www.pcworld.com/article/3179646/reddits-grand-vision-come-for-the-cats-stay-for-the-empathy.html.

10. For example, Meredith Woerner, "The Epic Mural of the Internet Doesn't Have Nearly Enough Cats," *io9* (blog), Gizmodo, January 29, 2010, https://io9.gizmodo.com/the-epic-mural-of-the-internet-doesnt-have-nearly-enoug-5459303. Adrienne Massanari begins her book on Reddit with a similarly casual reference: "If the internet is made of cats, reddit.com (reddit) is its temple . . . I am sure I started visiting it semi-regularly in 2008/2009, mostly for the cat pictures. . . . I came to reddit because of the cats. I stayed for the community." Adrienne Lynne Massanari, *Participatory Culture, Community, and Play: Learning from Reddit* (New York: Peter Lang, 2015), 5.

11. See also Caroline O'Donovan, "They Put the U in UGC: BuzzFeed Builds a Community Vertical as a Talent Incubator," *NiemanLab*, May 20, 2013, http://www.niemanlab.org/2013/05/they-put-the-u-in-ugc-buzzfeed-builds-a-community-vertical-as-a-talent-incubator/.

12. "About BuzzFeed Community," BuzzFeed Community, accessed November 26, 2019, https://www.buzzfeed.com/community/about#catpower.

13. Quoc V. Le et al., "Building High-Level Features Using Large Scale Unsupervised Learning," in *Proceedings of the 29th International Conference on Machine Learning* (Edinburgh, Scotland: Omnipress, 2012), https://icml.cc/2012/papers/73.pdf.

14. John Markoff, "How Many Computers to Identify a Cat? 16,000," *New York Times*, June 26, 2012. See also Liat Clark, "Google's Artificial Brain Learns to Recognize Cat Videos,"

Wired, June 26, 2012, https://www.wired.com/2012/06/google-x-neural-network/.

15. Sarah Boxer, "Internet's Best Friend (Let Me Count the Ways)," *New York Times*, July 30, 2005, https://www.nytimes.com/2005/07/30/arts/internets-best-friend-let-me-count-the-ways.html.

16. John Blackstone, "Cats Take over Internet, Marketing World," *CBS News*, September 2, 2013, https://www.cbsnews.com/video/cat-videos-take-over-internet-marketing-world/.

17. john st., "Catvertising," *YouTube*, November 10, 2011, https://www.youtube.com/watch?v=IkOQw96cfyE.

18. Ethan Zuckerman, "Cute Cats to the Rescue? Participatory Media and Political Expression," in *Youth, New Media, and Political Participation*, eds. Danielle Allen and Jennifer Light (Boston: MIT Press), 131–54.

19. Kate Miltner, "SRSLY Phenomenal: An Investigation into the Appeal of Lolcats" (master's thesis, London School of Economics, 2011).

20. Eppink, "How Cats Took Over the Internet." Exhibition at the Museum of the Moving Image, New York City, 2015. This exhibition's account of the rise of the internet cat emphasizes technological factors: for example, the fact that cats are good subjects for the stationary cameras attached to personal computers. This book will place more emphasis on cultural factors.

21. Gideon Lewis Kraus, "In Search of the Heart of the Online Cat-Industrial Complex," *Wired,* August 31, 2012.

22. Dick Hebdige, *Subculture: The Meaning of Style* (New York: Routledge, [1979] 2013), 105.

23. Sara Kiesler, "The Hidden Messages in Computer Networks," *Harvard Business Review*, January 1986, https://hbr.org/1986/01/the-hidden-messages-in-computer-networks.

24. Suzanne Keller, "Foreword," in Starr Roxanne Hiltz and Murray Turoff, *The Network Nation: Human Communication Via Computer* (Reading, MA: Addison-Wesley, 1978), xix.

25. For example, one early study of communication on corporate computer bulletin boards "found that decision-making actually took longer over computer networks, even when the time spent typing was taken into account, and that uninhibited behavior (insults and anger) increased." Cited in Jennifer Jean McGee, "Net of a Million Lies: Rhetoric and Community on Three Usenet Newsgroups" (PhD diss., University of Minnesota, 1998), 12. As late as 1995, Nancy Baym could report of scholarship on computer-mediated communication that "task-oriented applications of CMC remain the focus of most research." Nancy Baym, "The Emergence of Community in Computer-Mediated Communication," in *CyberSociety: Computer-Mediated Communication and Community*, ed. Steven Jones (Thousand Oaks, CA: Sage Publications, 1995), 139.

26. Hiltz and Turoff, *The Network Nation*, 62, 88, 96–113.

27. Ibid., 76–83.

28. Howard Rheingold, *The Virtual Community: Homesteading on the Electronic Frontier* (Reading, MA: Addison-Wesley, 1993), 54–56.

29. Michael Mahoney, "The Histories of Computing(s)," *Interdisciplinary Science Reviews* 30, no. 2 (2005): 119.

30. See, for example, Fred Turner, From Counterculture to Cyberculture: Stewart Brand, the Whole Earth Network, and the Rise of Digital Utopianism (Chicago: The University of Chicago Press, 2006); Jonathan Zittrain, The Future of the Internet and How to Stop It (New Haven, CT: Yale University Press, 2008).

31. See, for example, Scarlett Kilcooley-O'Halloran, "J Lo Responsible for Google Images," *Vogue.co.uk*, April 8, 2015,

https://www.vogue.co.uk/article/j-lo-green-versace-dress -responsible-for-google-image-search.

32. Jean Burgess and Joshua Green describe several competing narratives of YouTube's rise in *YouTube* (Cambridge, UK: Polity Press, 2009), 2–4. For examples of this particular narrative in action, see John Biggs, "A Video Clip Goes Viral, and a TV Network Wants to Control It," *New York Times*, February 20, 2006, https://www.nytimes.com/2006/02/20/business/media/a -video-clip-goes-viral-and-a-tv-network-wants-to-control-it .html; and Andrew Wallenstein and Todd Spangler, "'Lazy Sunday' Turns 10: 'SNL' Stars Recall How TV Invaded the Internet," *Variety*, December 18, 2015, https://variety.com/2015/tv/news/ lazy-sunday-10th-anniversary-snl-1201657949/.

1. Brian Clark Howard, "People Are Scaring Their Cats with Cucumbers. They Shouldn't," *National Geographic*, November 17, 2015, https://www.nationalgeographic.com/news/2015/11/151117 -cats-cucumbers-videos-behavior/.

2. The *Gawker* journalist Adrian Chen later claimed that he started the fad of cat breading in order to drive up traffic at *Gawker* by creating a viral phenomenon. Adrian Chen, Twitter post, August 17, 2015, https://twitter.com/adrianchen/status/63 3472532981678080?lang=en; Adrien Chen, "Hot New Internet Meme: 'Breading' Cats," *Gawker* (January 31, 2012), https:// gawker.com/5880885/hot-new-internet-meme-breading-cats; Kaitlyn Tiffany, "If You Want to Make a Meme, You Have to Break a Few Journalists," *The Verge* (August 18, 2015), https:// www.theverge.com/2015/8/18/9171755/meme-gawker-buzzfeed -cat-bread-breading-make-your-own.

3. Black Metal Cats (@evilbmcats).

4. I suspect that, at least some of the time, this is a film-maker's joke about a famous screenwriting book called *Save the Cat*. Blake Snyder, *Save the Cat! The Last Screening Writing Book You'll Ever Need* (Studio City, CA: M. Wiese, 2005).

5. See Robert Darnton, *The Great Cat Massacre: And Other Episodes in French Cultural History* (New York: Basic Books, [1984] 2009).

6. Ibid., xviii.

7. I refer here only to the European context. For the meanings of cats before the Middle Ages, and a brief discussion of why those meanings changed, see Donald W. Engels, *Classical Cats: The Rise and Fall of the Sacred Cat* (New York: Routledge, 1999).

8. Ibid., 95. Thus, for example, a French historical diction-ary gives the slang meaning of *chat* (literally *cat*) as follows: "*CHAT. Sexe de la femme. Synonyme: la chatte.*" (The dictionary also gives as an example sentence, marked as obscene, "Je lui ai mange la chatte"—i.e., "I ate her pussy.") See John F. Moffitt, "Provocative Felinity in Manet's 'Olympia,'" *Source: Notes in the History of Art* 14, no. 1 (Fall 1994): 27–28.

9. After I had spent some time around cats, I noticed that the cat in Boucher's painting is wearing an expression that says, "Let's play." To my mind, this at least confirms that Boucher owned a cat.

10. P. Reuterswärd, "The Dog in the Humanist's Study," *Konsthistorisk Tidskrift* 50, no. 2 (1981): 54–57.

11. Moffitt, "Provocative Felinity in Manet's 'Olympia,'" 21–25.

12. Because dogs are good trackers, and may seem to use subtle wit to track, dogs sometimes served in medieval and early modern art as representations of wit or acumen. Reuter-swärd, "The Dog in the Humanist's Study," 56–57.

13. The name of the dead cat changes from telling to telling. I used the name Grimalkin for illustrative purposes.

14. John Lindow, "Cats and Dogs, Trolls and Devils: At Home in Some Migratory Legend Types," *Western Folklore* 69, no. 2 (Spring 2010): 163–79.

15. The 17th-century author Charles Perrault gave this story its modern name and fame. Per his usual fashion, Perrault gave the story two morals, one suited to children and one suited to adults. Loosely translated, the first was *diligence can be worth more, in the end, than a great inheritance*, while the second was *clothes make the man.*

16. Claude Levi-Strauss, *Totemism,* trans. Rodney Needham (Boston: Beacon Press, [1962] 1963), 89.

17. Quoted in Desmond Morris, *Catlore* (New York: Crown Publishers, 1987), 158–59. The first novel-length horror story to appear, in English, in print had the title "Beware the Cat." William Baldwin, "A Marvelous Hystory Intituled, Beware the Cat" (London: At the Long Shop Adioyning Unto Saint Mildreds Church in the Pultrie by Edward Allde, [1553] 1584). Accessed on Early English Books Online.

18. Casey Chan, "Why Do Cats Die Funny and Dogs Die Sad in Movies?" *Gizmodo*, August 5, 2016, https://gizmodo.com/and-i-don-t-blame-it-for-wanting-to-survive-1784945261?jwsource=cl.

19. *New York Daily News*, October 8, 2016.

20. See, for example, David Alan Grier, *When Computers Were Human* (Princeton, NJ: Princeton University Press, 2005); N. Katherine Hayles, *My Mother Was a Computer: Digital Subjects and Literary Texts* (Chicago: The University of Chicago Press, 2005); and Marie Hicks, *Programmed Inequality: How Britain Discarded Women Technologists and Lost Its Edge in Computing* (Cambridge, MA: MIT Press, 2017).

21. Vannevar Bush, "As We May Think," *The Atlantic,* July 1945, https://www.theatlantic.com/magazine/archive/1945/07/as-we-may-think/303881/.

22. According to Grier, this may have been John Tukey, the creator of the word *bit* for *binary digit*. The Bell Labs researcher George Stibitz made similar use of the term *girl years* (Grier, *When Computers Were Human*, 365ff).

23. Starr Roxanne Hiltz and Murray Turoff, *The Network Nation: Human Communication Via Computer* (Reading, MA: Addison-Wesley, 1978), 13.

24. On the origins of hacker culture at MIT, see, for example, Steven Levy, *Hackers: Heroes of the Computer Revolution* (New York: Doubleday, [1984] 1994).

25. Howard Rheingold, *The Virtual Community: Homesteading on the Electronic Frontier* (Reading, MA: Addison-Wesley, 1993),, 49. In 1991, a journalist wrote in a dispatch from a conference dedicated to personal workstation computers, still a novelty to mainstream culture: "They call themselves MacAddicts. They are hard-core users of the Apple Macintosh personal computer, and they've come to San Francisco by the tens of thousands for their annual tribal gathering, the Macworld Expo. Some have on suits and carry briefcases. Some have on Grateful Dead T-shirts and carry briefcases. More than a few of them look MacStoned." Walter Kirn, "Valley of the Nerds," *Gentleman's Quarterly*, July 1991, 97.

26. Indeed, a Grateful Dead lyricist, John Perry Barlow, was a prominent early theorist of cyberspace. See, for example, John Perry Barlow, "A Declaration of Independence for Cyberspace," February 8, 1996, Electronic Frontier Foundation, https://www.eff.org/cyberspace-independence; and Turner, *From Counterculture to Cyberculture*, 171–74. Barlow founded the Electronic Frontier Foundation in collaboration with Mitchell Kapor.

27. Levy, *Hackers*, 139–42.

28. Studies of the relationship between computer culture and the hippie counterculture, in particular, include Turner,

From Counterculture to Cyberculture; and John Markoff, *What the Dormouse Said: How the Sixties Counterculture Shaped the Personal Computer Industry* (New York: Penguin Books, 2005).

29. We can find an example of a writer using the word *punk* with its original meaning in Percival Stockdale's 1778 poem "An Elegy on The Death of Dr. Johnson's Favourite Cat":

> [The cat's] example we shall find
> A keen reproof of human kind.
> He lived in town, yet ne'er got drunk,
> Nor spent one farthing on a punk . . .

On *punk* as military slang, see Elbridge Colby's military glossary, *Army Talk: A Familiar Dictionary of Soldier Speech* (Princeton, NJ: Princeton University Press, 1942).

30. Gordon Meyer and Jim Thomas, "The Baudy World of the Byte Bandit: A Postmodernist Interpretation of the Computer Underground," *Gordon's Desktop Publications*, June 10, 1990, http://hacker.textfiles.com/papers/baudy.html. Broadly speaking, *hacking* means taking unauthorized access of computers. In the 1960s and 1970s, the term *hacker* mostly referred to computer geeks. In the 1980s, new attention to the activities of hackers who tried to access computer systems belonging to government and industry changed the meaning of the word in popular culture. For most hackers, the term *hacking* refers to the practice of mastering, exploring, or playing around with computers. Ibid.

31. Ibid.; Thomas J. Holt, "Hacks, Cracks, and Crime: An Examination of the Subculture and Social Organization of Computer Hackers" (PhD diss., University of Missouri-St. Louis, 2005), 11–28.

32. Quoted in Dick Hebdige's brilliant and classic work on punk style, *Subculture: The Meaning of Style (New York: Routledge, [1979] 2013)*, 105, 109–10. Hebdige also comments on Umberto Eco's melodrama.

33. See, for example, Meyer and Thomas, "The Baudy World of the Byte Bandit"; Elizabeth M. Reid, "Electropolis: Communication and Community on Internet Relay Chat" (honors thesis, University of Melbourne, 1991); and Paul Taylor, *Hackers: Crime in the Digital Sublime* (London: Routledge, 1999), 169–70.

34. I am aware that someone may reply that punk is itself postmodern.

35. Dave Grohl, the drummer for the band Nirvana—which Grohl and Kurt Cobain described as punk, not "grunge"—later recalled recognizing the political possibilities of DIY culture as an adolescent: "More than the noise and the rebellion and the danger, it was the blissful removal of these bands from any source of conventional, popular, corporate structure and the underground network that supported the music's independence that was totally inspiring to me. At thirteen years old, I realized I could start my own band, I could write my own song, I could record my own record, I could start my own label, I could release my own record, I could book my own shows, I could write and publish my own fanzine, I could silk-screen my own tee shirts— I could do this all by myself. There was no right or wrong, because it was all mine." Dave Grohl, keynote speech, South by Southwest festival, 2013, https://www.rollingstone.com/music/music-news/dave-grohls-sxsw-keynote-speech-the-complete-text-89152/.

36. Hebdige, *Subculture*, 120–21.

37. Levy, *Hackers*, 26–36. This ethos is outlined, for example, in the Jargon File, an unofficial document (there are no official documents in this sphere) that defines a hacker in seven ways: a hacker takes pleasure in exploring computer systems; a hacker is a practitioner of programming, not merely a theorist; a hacker programs quickly and well; a hacker has expertise in a specific program or works on it often; a hacker can appreciate

work put toward an outwardly useless purpose; a hacker is a buff or expert in any domain, not just computing; a hacker takes pleasure in mastering any kind of limitation. The Jargon File adds one "incorrect" definition: a hacker explores a system in order to acquire protected information. "The correct term for this sense is cracker." "Hacker," The Jargon File, version 4.4.8, http://www.catb.org/jargon/html/H/hacker.html. Cited in Holt, "Hacks, Cracks, and Crime," 6.

38. Meyer and Thomas, "The Baudy World of the Byte Bandit." Hackers also did boundary maintenance by circulating, and mocking, news stories about hackers in the mainstream media that got hacking wrong, for instance by construing all computer activity to be criminal. In 1984, the *Washington Post* described hacker communities using these terms: "Using long-distance telephone lines that they break into by duplicating telephone company tones . . . the hackers log onto each other's underground 'bulletin boards' to trade surreptitiously obtained corporate telephone numbers and passwords, or post valid credit card numbers, or carry on silent computer-screen conversations at hours when good high school students are supposed to be in bed." It's easy to understand why this was considered fake news, since it wasn't illegal to piggyback on telephone lines—"break into" the lines, in the *Post*'s alarmist term.

39. Bronwen Calvert, "William Gibson's 'Cyberpunk' *X-Files*," *Science Fiction Film and Television* 6, no. 1 (2013): 39–53. We may see residues of punk culture even in the deliberate misspellings and verbal infelicities that characterize the insider language of "the internetz." As Hebdige observes, *zines*, or privately printed magazines about punk culture, had a distinctive style: they were weird, oddball, personal, calculatedly nonprofessional. "The language in which the various manifestoes were framed was determinedly 'working class' (i.e., it was liberally peppered with swear words) and typing errors and

grammatical mistakes, misspellings and jumbled pagination were left uncorrected in the final proof. . . . The overwhelming impression was one of urgency and immediacy, of a paper produced in indecent haste, of memos from the front line" (Hebdige, *Subculture*, 111–12). Early hacker zines published online, like *Phrack*, share much of this aesthetic. It seems likely that some of the shibboleths of webspeak—I once saw a tweet that read, "anyone on twitter who uses uppercase is a cop"—ultimately trace back to the punk zine aesthetic.

40. After all, digital communication often reads as terse and aggressive, lacking as it does the context cues of face-to-face communication. On definitions of computer-mediated communication, see, for example, Pixy Ferris, "What Is CMC? An Overview of Scholarly Definitions," *CMC Magazine*, January 1997; and Susan Herring, "Computer-Mediated Discourse," in *The Handbook of Discourse Analysis*, eds. Deborah Schiffrin, Deborah Tannen, and Heidi E. Hamilton (Oxford: Blackwell, 2003), 612–34. On definitions of trolling in the context of computer-mediated communication, see, for example, Claire Hardaker, "Trolling in Asynchronous Computer-Mediated Communication: From User Discussions to Academic Definitions," *Journal of Politeness Research* 6, no. 2 (2010): 215–42.

41. Meyer and Thomas, "The Baudy World of the Byte Bandit"; Holt, "Hacks, Cracks, and Crime," 74–82.

42. See, for example, Lori Kendall, Hanging Out in the Virtual Pub: Masculinities and Relationships Online (Berkeley: University of California Press, 2002); T. L. Taylor, Raising the Stakes: E-Sports and the Professionalization of Computer Gaming (Cambridge, MA: MIT Press, 2012), 112–17; and Megan Condis, "'Get Raped, F****t': Trolling as a Gendered Metagame," in Gaming Masculinity: Trolls, Fake Geeks, and the Gendered Battle for Online Culture (Iowa City: University of Iowa Press, 2018), 20–21.

CHAPTER 2

1. Dave Barry, *Dave Barry in Cyberspace* (New York: Crown Publishing Group, 1996); John Seabrook, *Deeper: My Two-Year Odyssey in Cyberspace* (New York: Simon and Schuster, 1997); Julian Dibbell, *My Tiny Life: Crime and Passion in a Virtual World* (New York: Henry Holt and Company, 1998). Some of that naïveté was feigned, some not. After he received a rude email message, Seabrook wrote to CompuServe to ask, indignantly, "whether their subscribers were allowed" to engage in name-calling (102–103).

2. Usenet subscribers used the term "Eternal September" to describe the period, starting in September 1993, when AOL made Usenet available to its subscribers and thus the period in which Usenet belonged to the general public rather than the initiated few. The clock could never be turned back. Walter Isaacson, *The Innovators: How a Group of Hackers, Geniuses, and Geeks Created the Digital Revolution* (New York: Simon and Schuster, 2014): 401.

3. Seabrook, *Deeper*, 103–105.

4. Ibid., 104.

5. For reports from the front lines of present-day trolling, see, for example, Whitney Phillips, *This Is Why We Can't Have Nice Things: Mapping the Relationship between Online Trolling and Mainstream Culture* (Cambridge, MA: MIT Press, 2015); Angela Nagle, *Kill All Normies:_Online Culture Wars from 4Chan and Tumblr to Trump and the Alt-Right* (London: Zero Books, 2017); and other sources cited below. In cases like the cat newsgroup invasion, the practice of trolling overlaps with that of *flaming*, or posting hostile and offensive content. Incidentally, an early subgenre of flaming on Usenet was bombarding a newsgroup with instances of the word *meow*, a practice that originated in the newgroup alt.flame. "Apparently one of

the regular posters to alt.flame had a tendency to replace many of his words with 'meow,' à la Henrietta Pussycat in Mr. Rogers' Neighborhood. When it was discovered that this irritated a lot of people, a group of 'meowers' began posting long messages consisting entirely of 'meows' to newsgroups." Jennifer Jean McGee, "Net of a Million Lies: Rhetoric and Community on Three Usenet Newsgroups" (PhD diss., University of Minnesota, 1998), 173ff.

6. See, for example, Josh Quittner, "The War between alt.tasteless and rec.pets.cats," *Wired*, May 1, 1994, https://www.wired.com/1994/05/alt-tasteless/; Stephanie Brail, "The Price of Admission: Harassment and Free Speech in the Wild, Wild West," in *Wired Women: Gender and New Realities in Cyberspace*, eds. Lynn Cherry and Elizabeth Reba Weise (Toronto: Seal Press, 1996), 141–57; and Caitlin Dewey, "Meet the Internet's Earliest Cat Lovers—and the Trolls Who Terrorized Them," *Washington Post*, August 8, 2014, https://www.washingtonpost.com/news/the-intersect/wp/2014/08/08/meet-the-internets-earliest-cat-lovers-and-the-trolls-who-terrorized-them/.

7. Robert Darnton, The Great Cat Massacre: And Other Episodes in French Cultural History (New York: Basic Books, [1984] 2009), 100.

8. Quittner, "The War between alt.tasteless and rec.pets.cats."

9. In a well-publicized incident in 2017, Harvard University revoked the acceptances of several admitted, but not yet enrolled, teenagers who had joined a Facebook group for Harvard's class of 2021 and then created a private messaging group, titled "Harvard Memes for Horny Bourgeois Teens," where they traded memes and jokes that made light of "the Holocaust, child abuse, sexual assault, as well as posts that denigrated minority groups." Rebecca Heilweil, "Harvard Rescinds

Admissions to 10 Students for Offensive Facebook Memes," *Forbes*, January 5, 2017, https://www.forbes.com/sites/rebecca heilweil1/2017/06/05/harvard-rescinds-10-admissions-offer-for -offensive-facebook-memes-ollowing-commencement-speaker -zuckerberg/#3dc579473dbd.

10. Among players of League of Legends, for example, rumors abound that the game's creator, Riot Games, maintains separate servers to which trolls can be banished, and the game company Blizzard Entertainment has suggested that it has experimented with quarantine procedures for trolls. Steve Schirra, User Experience Research Manager at Twitch, Facebook direct message to the author, January 23, 2019; Yannick LeJacq, "How Blizzard Is Taking Aim at Toxic Players in Heroes of the Storm," *Kotaku*, March 6, 2015, https://www.kotaku.co.uk/2015/ 03/05/blizzard-taking-aim-toxic-players-heroes-storm.

11. As John Synnott and Marla Ioannou noted in 2017, "studies of group trolling" have been rare in the literature on trolling in comparison with studies of the behavior and motivations of individual trolls. John Synnott and Marla Ioannou, "Online Trolling: The Case of Madeleine McCann," *Computers in Human Behavior* 71 (January 2017): 72.

12. Quittner, "The War between alt.tasteless and rec.pets .cats."

13. For example, the term *sootikin*, which was in sufficiently heavy circulation in the newsgroup to appear in the newsgroup's FAQ. I won't define the term here, but it involves a definite misunderstanding of female anatomy. Cited in Quittner, "The War between alt.tasteless and rec.pets.cats."

14. Ibid.

15. Brail, "The Price of Admission," 152.

16. Quittner, "The War between alt.tasteless and rec.pets. cats." See also Dewey, "Meet the Internet's Earliest Cat Lovers—and the Trolls Who Terrorized Them."

17. Darnton, *The Great Cat Massacre*, 98. A typical cri de coeur from a cat owner is Samantha Paige Rosen, "I Have Three Cats, but Don't Call Me a Crazy Cat Lady," *Washington Post*, May 30, 2016, https://www.washingtonpost.com/news/soloish/wp/2016/05/30/i-have-three-cats-but-dont-call-me-a-crazy-cat-lady/.

18. "Introduction," *Witchcraft in England, 1558–1618*, ed. Barbara Rosen (Amherst: The University of Massachusetts Press, [1969] 1991), 32.

19. Darnton, *The Great Cat Massacre*, 96. As Barbara Rosen and James Serpell note, though churchmen throughout early modern Europe believed that witches had dubious relationships with animals, only the English gave plentiful accounts of *animal familiars*, or companion animals that were demons in disguise. Continental witches mainly rode demons in the shape of animals to Witches' Sabbaths or paid obeisance to the Devil while he was in animal form. We can attribute this difference, Serpell suggests, to the mock-clerical image of witchcraft on the Continent, where witches, who purportedly practiced witchcraft as a systematic inversion of Church practice, worked in corporate bodies, not in solitude. English witchcraft was by reputation the province of isolated miscreants—widows and spinsters, whose very solitude, and efforts to ease that solitude with animal companionship, could be pathologized. Rosen, "Introduction"; James Serpell, "Guardian Spirits or Demonic Pets: The Concept of the Witch's Familiar in Early Modern England, 1530–1712," in A.N.H. Craeger and W. C. Jordan. Rochester, eds., *The Animal–Human Boundary: Historical Perspectives* (Rochester, NY: Rochester University Press, 2002): 159–82. On the persecution of people with companion animals as witches, see also Keith Thomas, *Man and the Natural World: Changing Attitudes in England, 1500–1800* (Oxford: Oxford University Press, [1983] 1996); and James Serpell, *In the Company of*

Animals: A Study of Human-Animal Relationships (Cambridge: Cambridge University Press, [1986] 1996).

20. Brail, "The Price of Admission," 152.

21. Quittner, "The War between alt.tasteless and rec.pets.cats."

22. Geoffrey Hughes, "Slang," in An Encyclopedia of Swearing: The Social History of Oaths, Profanity, Foul Language, and Ethnic Slurs in the English-Speaking World (New York: Routledge, [2006] 2015), 438.

23. Phillips, This Is Why We Can't Have Nice Things, 62.

24. Brail, "The Price of Admission," 152.

25. Quittner, "The War between alt.tasteless and rec.pets.cats." Anecdotes like these are familiar features of news stories about trolling in our own time, which have described trolls sending death and rape threats, altering images to portray victims in grisly crime scenes, and publicizing the home addresses of victims. See, for example, Karla Mantilla, *Gendertrolling: How Misogyny Went Viral* (Santa Barbara, CA: Praeger, 2015); and Megan Condis, "'Get Raped, F****t': Trolling as a Gendered Metagame," in *Gaming Masculinity: Trolls, Fake Geeks, and the Gendered Battle for Online Culture* (Iowa City: University of Iowa Press, 2018), 31–33.

26. See, for example, Christine Cook, Juliette Schaafsma, and Marjolijn Antheunis, "Under the Bridge: An In-Depth Examination of Online Trolling in the Gaming Context," *New Media and Society* 20, no. 9 (2018): 3323; Mantilla, *Gendertrolling;* and Condis, "'Get Raped, F****t'," 15–37.

27. Today, researchers disagree about exactly what constitutes trolling. As Christine Cook et al. note in a 2018 study of trolls in gaming, "despite its prevalence in cyberspace, trolling as a subject of academic study is a confusing space, with different researchers using different criteria to describe the same phenomenon. This is likely due to the fact that it is such a new field of study: existing studies are few and far between, and

nearly all of them have been atheoretical due to a lack of empirical basis upon which to build any theories" ("Under the Bridge," 3324).

28. Michele Tepper, "Usenet Communities and the Cultural Politics of Communication," in *Internet Culture*, ed. David Porter (New York: Routledge, 1997), 39–54.

29. Within a few decades, internet users recognized trolling to be a serious social problem, in large part because trolling had come by then to encompass a range of hostile and destructive behaviors. See, for example, Jonathan Bishop, "Representations of 'Trolls' in Mass Media Communication: A Review of Media-Texts and Moral Panics Relating to 'Internet Trolling,'" *International Journal of Web Based Communities* 10, no. 1 (2014): 7–24. Also see Emma Jane's discussion of "e-bile," an umbrella term that she uses for trolling, flaming, and other forms of online hostility: Emma A. Jane, "Flaming? What Flaming? The Pitfalls and Potentials of Researching Online Hostility," *Ethics and Information Technology* 17, no. 1 (March 2015): 65.

30. For early discussions of alt.folklore.urban, see, for example, Jan Harold Brumvard, *The Baby Train and Other Lusty Urban Legends* (New York: W.W. Norton & Company, 1994), especially 191–94; Alice Dragoon, "True Lies," *CIO 8* (April 15, 1995): 22–24; and Joseph M. Saul, "Myths Spread Quickly in the Information Age," *Information Technology Digest 5*, no. 2, February 12, 1996, 1, 12–14).

31. "How the Truth Set Snopes Free," Webby Awards website, https://www.webbyawards.com/lists/how-the-truth-set-snopes-free/.

32. Tepper, "Usenet Communities and the Cultural Politics of Communication," 48.

33. Julian Dibbell, "A Rape in Cyberspace: Or, How an Evil Clown, a Haitian Trickster Spirit, Two Wizards, and a Cast of

Dozens Turned a Database into a Society," *Village Voice*, December 21, 1993; republished in Dibbel, *My Tiny Life: Crime and Passion in a Virtual World* (New York: Henry Holt and Company, 1998), 11–32.

34. See, for example, Jill Sternberg, *Misbehavior in Cyber Places: The Regulation of Online Conduct in Virtual Communities on the Internet* (Lanham, MD: University Press of America, 2012), especially 79–81.

35. Tepper, "Usenet Communities and the Cultural Politics of Communication," 40–42.

36. Ibid., 39–43.

37. Ibid., 39–40.

38. Ibid., 40.

39. Ibid., 41.

40. Ibid.

41. Ibid., 42–43.

42. Ibid.

43. Ibid., 50.

44. Cook et al., "Under the Bridge," 3334–35.

CHAPTER 3

1. Scholarly discussions of memes were also late arrivals. One of the first academic books to focus on memes is Limor Schifman, *Memes in Digital Culture* (Cambridge, MA: MIT Press, 2013). Ryan Milner's *The World Made Meme: Public Conversations and Participatory Media* (Cambridge, MA: MIT Press, 2016) followed a few years later. Milner discusses the difference between memes and viral content (37–39). The term *meme* originated in Richard Dawkins, *The Selfish Gene* (Oxford: Oxford University Press, 1976); Dawkins used the term to refer to a cultural element that reproduces itself as humans pass it along through imitation.

2. Cole Stryker, *Epic Win for Anonymous: An Online Army Conquers the Media* (New York: Overlook Duckworth, 2011), 130. Nashimura turned 23 the year 2channel began, but he was born in November and 2channel began in May. The threads on 2channel can cover a range of topics, as Stryker notes (132–33).

3. Lisa Katayama, "Meet Hiroyuki Nashimura, the Bad Boy of the Japanese Internet," *Wired*, May 19, 2008, https://www.wired.com/2008/05/mf-hiroyuki/.

4. Katayama, "Meet Hiroyuki Nashimura." Katayama notes, "There's also a prankish streak: When fast-food chain Lotteria held an online poll asking customers to vote for a new flavor of milk shake, 2channelers stuffed the ballot box in favor of kimchi—fermented cabbage."

5. Stryker, *Epic Win for Anonymous*, 130–33. I am grateful to William Fleming, a scholar of Japanese culture at the University of California, Santa Barbara, for translations and advice.

6. "2 Channel," Syberpunk, Internet Archive, December 5, 2004, https://web.archive.org/web/20041205002432/http:/www.syberpunk.com:80/cgi-bin/index.pl?page=2ch. The writer also notes the existence of several spinoff boards, including World 2ch, "for international users," and 2chan, which had image boards so that users could see images rather than merely talk.

7. Nobody is certain when cats first arrived in Japan. Cats appear in the 11th-century text *The Tale of Genji*—the world's first novel, written by the court lady Murasaki Shikibu. In the novel, when a court lady rebuffs the affections of a man of the court, he steals her cat and displaces his feelings for her onto the cat, making it a fetish object. In this instance, the cat straightforwardly stands in for female genitalia—the man even has a dream about romancing the cat—but the Japanese language doesn't have a pun that connects genitalia and cats directly, as many European languages do. Cats may have come to Japan along trade routes that led to Egypt or China; they

may have been aristocratic gifts, or they may have accompanied monks who wanted to protect their silk scrolls from mice.
Zack Davisson, *Kaibyō: The Supernatural Cats of Japan* (Seattle
and Portland, OR: Chin Music Press and Mercuria Press,
2017), 21–22.

8. Davisson, *Kaibyō*, 15–18.

9. Ibid., 26–28.

10. These images were the subject of a 2015 exhibit at the
Japan Society in New York City. See "Life of Cats: Selections
from the Hiraki Ukiyo-e Collection," Japan Society, https://
www.japansociety.org/page/programs/gallery/life-of-cats.

11. Ibid., 22–26.

12. Vyvyan Evans, *The Emoji Code: The Linguistics behind
Smiley Faces and Scaredy Cats* (New York: Picador, 2017),
10–20. As Evans notes (148–49), the idea of an emoticon, or a
set of typed characters representing a face, has been invented
out of whole cloth several times. For example, such an item
appears in an 1881 issue of the British humor magazine *Puck*;
and while writing to a *New York Times* reporter in 1969, Vladi-
mir Nabokov rebuffed an impolite question (how he ranked
himself among writers) by saying, "I often think there should
exist a special typographical sign for a smile—some sort of
concave mark, a supine round bracket, which I would now like
to trace in reply to your question." The first digital smiley face
on record appears in a post that Scott E. Fahlman, a professor
of computer science at Carnegie Mellon University, made to a
Carnegie Mellon bulletin board in 1982. Following up on a
case in which a facetious post had been taken as truth, Fahlman made the following tongue-in-cheek proposal:

> I propose that the following character sequence for joke
> markers
>
> :-)

Read it sideways. Actually, it is probably more economical to mark things that are NOT jokes, given current trends. For this, use

:-(

13. Ibid., 18–20. To view the original set of emojis, see, for example, Paul Galloway, "The Original NTT DOCOMO Emoji Set Has Been Added to the Museum of Modern Art's Collection," Museum of Modern Art, October 26, 2016, https://stories.moma.org/the-original-emoji-set-has-been -added-to-the-museum-of-modern-arts-collection-c6060e141f61.

14. Stryker, *Epic Win for Anonymous*, 141; Taylor Wofford, "Fuck You and Die: An Oral History of Something Awful," *Motherboard* (blog), *Vice*, April 5, 2017, https://www.vice.com/ en_us/article/nzg4yw/fuck-you-and-die-an-oral-history-of -something-awful.

15. Stryker, *Epic Win for Anonymous*, 141–48.

16. On the comedic styles of Weird Twitter and Vine, see, for example, Elyse Graham, "We Like Short Shorts," *Public Books*, April 17, 2018.

17. Wofford, "Fuck You and Die."

18. Ibid.

19. Personal communication, Jason Eppink, January 20, 2019.

20. Stryker, *Epic Win for Anonymous*, 147–48.

21. See, for example, Henry Jenkins, *Textual Poachers: Television Fans and Participatory Culture* (New York: Routledge, 1992); Karine Nahon and Jeff Hemsley, *Going Viral* (New York: Polity, 2013); Adrienne Massanari, *Participatory Culture, Community, and Play: Learning from Reddit* (New York: Peter Lang, 2015); Nicholas John, *The Age of Sharing* (New York: Polity, 2017); and Whitney Phillips and Ryan Milner, *The Ambivalent Internet: Mischief, Oddity and Antagonism Online* (New York: Polity, 2017).

22. Stryker, *Epic Win for Anonymous*, 41–43.

23. Ibid., 80.

24. "Caturday," Chan4chan, archive tag, http://chan4chan .com/archive/tags/caturday_cat.

25. Lauren Gawne and Jill Vaughan, "I Can Haz Language Play: Construction of Language and Identity in LOLspeak," in *Proceedings of the 42nd Australian Linguistics Society Conference*, eds. M. Ponsonnet, L. Dao, and M. Bowler (Canberra: ANU Research, 2011): 102–03, 114. https://pdfs.semanticscholar.org/ cfb9/15fb2fb58834e7565796d11061bb0d49802b.pdf.

26. Stryker, Epic Win for Anonymous, 80.

27. Ibid., 125–26.

28. Stryker, Epic Win for Anonymous, 80.

29. Gawne and Vaughan, "I Can Haz Language Play," 111–12.

30. Hello Kitty's "biographical" name is "Kitty White." Christine Yano discusses the deliberate layering of Japanese and Anglo-American elements in the Hello Kitty brand in *Pink Globalization: Hello Kitty's Trek Across the Pacific* (Durham, NC: Duke University Press, 2013), 18–19.

31. 1992 and 1987 are the dates that the versions of the games with those specific translations were released. "A Winner Is You," Know Your Meme, https://knowyourmeme.com/memes/ a-winner-is-you (accessed January 3, 2020); "All Your Base Are Belong to Us," Know Your Meme, https://knowyourmeme .com/memes/all-your-base-are-belong-to-us (accessed January 3, 2020).

32. Douglas McGray, "Japan's Gross National Cool," *Foreign Policy*, November 11, 2009, https://foreignpolicy.com/2009/ 11/11/japans-gross-national-cool/.

33. Chi Hyun Park, in "Orientalism in U. S. Cyberpunk Cinema from *Blade Runner* to *The Matrix*" (PhD diss., University of Texas at Austin, 2004), 4, 139–56, 179–214. Park presents a meticulous catalog and discussion of Asian elements in sci-fi

and cyberpunk films. In his review of *The Matrix* for *Time* magazine, Jeffrey Ressner notes the influence of anime in the design of the film's fight scenes: "Never seen the mega-imaginative, ultraviolent Japanese cartoons known as *anime* (*Akira, Ghost in the Shell*)? Now you have—in whirling live action" (quoted in Park, "Orientalism," 183). Richard Corliss, "Popular Metaphysics," *Time*, April 11, 1999, http://www.whoaisnotme.net/articles/1999_0411_pop.htm.

34. Anne Allison, *Millennial Monsters: Japanese Toys and the Global Imagination* (Berkeley: University of California Press, 2006). On transmedia storytelling, see, for example, Henry Jenkins, *Convergence Culture: Where Old and New Media Collide* (New York: New York University Press, 2008).

35. Anne Allison, "Cuteness as Japan's Millennial Product," in *Pikachu's Global Adventure: The Rise and Fall of Pokémon*, ed. Tobin Joseph (Durham, NC: Duke University Press, 2004), 34–49. See also Anne Allison, "The Attractions of the J-Wave for American Youth," in *Soft Power Superpowers: Cultural and National Assets of Japan and the United States*, ed. Yasushi Watanabe and David L. McConnell (Armonk, NY: M. E. Sharpe, 2008), 99–110.

36. McGray, "Japan's Gross National Cool"; Allison, *Millennial Monsters*, 5–6.

37. Christoph Niemann, "Untitled," *New Yorker* cover, March 18, 2002. Cited in Allison, *Millennial Monsters*, 18.

38. Adrian Favell, Before and After Superflat: A Short History of Japanese Contemporary Art, 1990–2011 (Hong Kong: Blue Kingfisher, 2011), 41.

39. McGray, "Japan's Gross National Cool."

40. *Japonisme* marked the work of artists as diverse as Mary Cassatt, Edgar Degas, Édouard Manet, Henri Toulouse-Lautrec, Vincent Van Gogh, and James McNeill Whistler. See, for example, Klaus Berger, *Japonisme in Western Painting from*

Whistler to Matisse, trans. David Britt (Cambridge: Cambridge University Press, [1980] 1992). Berger takes care to emphasize that, in any thoughtful discussion of Japanese influences on Western art during this period, "The word 'Japanese' does not represent a single, static entity but something that, in itself, has undergone a long and varied evolution. Its various phases have influenced the West in very different ways. Japonisme is not one phenomenon but several: Katsushika Hosukai's influence differs from Utamaro's, and Utamaro's in turn differs widely from that of the artists discovered at a later stage: the Primitives, Hishikawa Moronobu or Kaigetsudo. There are many stylistic levels within Japanese art, to which the West responded in highly diverse ways. The word 'Japanese' meant something quite different to Édouard Manet from what it meant to Van Gogh, or to Henri de Toulouse-Lautrec, to Gustav Klimt or to George Grosz" (4).

41. Writes one scholar of 12th-century Japanese illustrations on narrative scrolls, "All have small, full, rounded faces that lack individuality; the eyes and heavy brows are straight ink lines, the noses simple hooks, the small rosebud lips are those of young girls. The style, called hikimekagihana ('dashes for eyes, hooks for noses') was a familiar device in the illustrations of romantic tales. . . . According to one theory, the very anonymity of the characters allowed viewers to identify themselves psychologically with the individuals portrayed in the paintings." Quoted in Yano, *Pink Globalization,* 21.

42. Ibid., 21. Yano is careful to identify this, not as a monolithic "aesthetic tradition," but as "a historically placed visual repertoire of meanings."

43. See, for example, Favell's brilliant *Before and After Superflat.*

44. Ibid., 64. See also, for example, Koichi Iwabuchi, *Recentering Globalization: Popular Culture and Japanese Transnationalism* (Durham, NC: Duke University Press, 2002).

45. Takashi Murakami, "The Super Flat Manifesto," in *Super Flat* (Madra, Tokyo, 2000), 5.

46. Quoted in Yano, *Pink Globalization*, 254–55.

47. Phillips and Milner, *The Ambivalent Internet*, 8.

48. Nick Douglas, "It's Supposed to Look Like Shit: The Internet Ugly Aesthetic," *Journal of Visual Culture* 13, no. 3 (2014): 314–39; Hebdige, *Subculture: The Meaning of Style* (New York: Routledge, [1979] 2013), 111.

49. Simon May discusses the politics of cuteness, with emphasis on American and Japanese culture, in *The Power of Cute* (Princeton, NJ: Princeton University Press, 2019). Another important recent analysis of cuteness as an aesthetic category—which does not, however, give much space to Japanese conceptions of cuteness—is Sianne Ngai, *Our Aesthetic Categories: Zany, Cute, Interesting* (Cambridge, MA: Harvard University Press, 2012).

50. Sharon Kinsella, "Cuties in Japan," in *Women, Media, and Consumption in Japan*, eds. Lise Skov and Brian Moeran (Richmond, UK: Curzon Press, 1995): 243–51. Of course, just as American corporations groomed teenagers as consumers by promoting consumption as a form of freedom, Japanese corporations promoted youth-oriented goods as symbols of freedom from adult responsibilities, which arguably eroded the rebellion that cute style represented. See Allison, "Cuteness as Japan's Millennial Product," 34–52; and John Whittier Treat, "Yoshimoto Banana Writes Home: The *Shōjo* in Japanese Popular Culture," *The Journal of Japanese Studies* 19, no. 2 (Summer 1993): 353–87.

51. The phrase "millennial Japonisme" is from Yano, *Pink Globalization*, 259. Yano argues that in the 2000s, Japan's soft-power policy, which translated the concept of Cool Japan as "Marketable, Youth-oriented, Feminine, Playful, Pop Japan," brought about the rise of a "world political economy of cute" (6–9).

52. Ibid., 57–58. Yano writes of the *kawaii* of Hello Kitty, for example: "Hello Kitty encompasses innocent childhood, on the one hand, and its own distancing commentary through clever, sly, even tongue-in-cheek, play, on the other. This perception stands in contrast to what [people] see as the straightforward, more unidimensional expression of American characters, such as Precious Moments (Christian-linked sentimentality) or Disney figures (often tied to specific narratives, such as blockbuster children's films)."

53. May describes elements that we might recognize as *kawaii* under the umbrella term "Uncanny Cute." He also offers a different reading of cute culture in Japan than do some of the other authors cited here: namely, that "the cult of Cute in Japan is . . . directly related to that great nation's will to convince itself and the world of its peaceful intentions." May, *The Power of Cute*, 25, 91.

54. Quoted in Kinsella, "Cuties in Japan," 220–21.

55. Yano, *Pink Globalization*, 57–58. Since the 1970s, one manifestation of *kawaii* culture has become especially pervasive in Japanese life: *kyarakutā*, or mascots that promote apps, airports, banks, cities, festivals, governments, police departments, television stations, temples, train lines, shopping districts, and more. (Brand characters such as Hello Kitty are also *kyarakutā*.) Peeping from buttons, clothes, handbags, keychains, mobile phones, watches, and other merchandise, these cuties render (or aim to render) the world softer, more intimate, more playful (11). Some observers view the mascots, meme characters, and digital surrogates that cluster on specific websites as digital *kyarakutā*. This would include official mascots like GitHub's "octocat" (a cross between an octopus and a cat), unofficial mascots like Fark's "Domo-kun chasing kittens" (a play on an actual Japanese *kyarakutā*), and memes like Business Cat, Long Cat, and Serious Cat.

56. Phillips and Milner, *The Ambivalent Internet*, 8–9.

57. Annalee Newitz, "What Makes Things Cheesy?: Satire, Multinationalism, and B-movies," *Social Text* 18, no. 2 (2000): 59–60.

58. Matt Hills, "Transcultural Otaku: Japanese Representations of Fandom and Representations of Japan in Anime/Manga Fan Cultures" (paper presented at the Media in Transition Conference, Massachusetts Institute of Technology, May 11, 2002), 1, 10–11, https://cmsw.mit.edu/mit2/Abstracts/Matt Hillspaper.pdf. See also Annalee Newitz, "Anime Otaku: Japanese Animation Fans Outside Japan," *Bad Subjects* 13 (1994): 1–12. Both Hills and Newitz include in the fan communities they discuss ethnically Japanese people living in the West.

59. Quoted in Hills, "Transcultural Otaku," 7.

60. Ibid., 4–5.

61. The writer of Syberpunk later wrote,

> I checked the counter on [Hokkaido's] site, and I was suprised [*sic*] at how very few visitors there had been to the site, about 2000 by my first count. It was then I realised this was an untouched website, probably only visited regularly by the owner and his friends in its 4 years on the net. I decided then to keep the site a secret, and I did for the next few months.
>
> Then I began sending a few friends this picture [Oolong with dorayaki on top of his head]. Many of you have probably seen it around before. It was my favourite picture, and despite my friends asking where I got it, I would not tell them. I wanted Oolong to remain a secret. Then one time I made the mistake of linking directly to the url of the picture at Oolongs website. From there the url was sent around, and people found out about the main site, and all the pictures. A few people posted links to Oolongs site on some

message boards, and from there it exploded. Oolong got over 150 thousand hits in just one week.

("Oolong," Syberpunk, Internet Archive, https://web.archive .org/web/20020607070235/http:/www.syberpunk.com:80/ cgi-bin/index.pl?page=oolong).

62. The *Oxford English Dictionary* dates the first source for the phrase *went viral* to 2001.

63. "Series 2," Syberpunk, Internet Archive, https://web .archive.org/web/20020606190204/http:/www.syberpunk .com:80/cgi-bin/index.pl?page=series2. The new Syberpunk blog displayed images of sophisticated cell phones; Pokémon-brand soft drinks; vitamin oral spray; an alarm clock that you could put over your ear while sleeping on the train; little tread-mills for your pets; "a crazy Japanese toilet." In 2004, Syber-punk reported on a Japanese message board called 2 Channel. Presumably many Western internet users learned about 2 Channel from such sources. "2 Channel," Syberpunk.

64. Sarah Boxer, "Prospecting for Gold among the Photo Blogs," *New York Times,* May 25, 2003, https://www.nytimes .com/2003/05/25/arts/art-architecture-prospecting-for-gold -among-the-photo-blogs.html; "Pancake Bunny," Know Your Meme, https://knowyourmeme.com/memes/pancake-bunny.

65. Stryker, *Epic Win for Anonymous,* 168. See also Daniel Terdiman, "The History of I Can Has Cheezburger," *cnet.com,* August 25, 2008, https://www.cnet.com/news/the-history-of-i -can-has-cheezburger/.

66. Stryker, *Epic Win for Anonymous,* 168. By August 2007, Huh's site reportedly had "around 200,000 unique visitors and a half- million page views each day." Aaron Rutkoff, "With 'Lolcats' Internet Fad, Anyone Can Get in on the Joke," *Wall Street Journal*, August 25, 2007, https://www.wsj.com/articles/ SB118798557326508182.

67. Stryker, *Epic Win for Anonymous,* 168–69. Huh's "Cheez-burger Network" of websites includes The Daily Squee, The Daily What, FAIL Blog, I Has a Hotdog, and Know Your Meme.

68. See, for example, Professor Happycat, *I Can Has Cheez-burger?: A Lolcat Collekshun* (New York: Gotham Books, 2008); Professor Happycat, *How 2 Take Over the Wurld: A Lolcat Guide to Winning* (New York: Gotham Books, 2009); Martin Grondin, *Lol Cat Bible: In teh Beginnin Ceiling Cat Maded the Skiez an da Earfs n Stuffs* (Berkeley, CA: Ulysses Press, 2010).

69. See Amy Farnsworth, "Lolcats Take to the Stage," *Christian Science Monitor,* August 14, 2009, https://www.csmonitor.com/Technology/Horizons/2009/0814/lolcats-take-to-the-stage-with-a-musical.

70. See, for example, Sarah Boxer, "Internet's Best Friend (Let Me Count the Ways)," *New York Times,* July 30, 2005, https://www.nytimes.com/2005/07/30/arts/internets-best-friend-let-me-count-the-ways.html; Tom Whitwell, "Micro-trends," *The Times* (London), May 12, 2007, https://www.thetimes.co.uk/article/microtrends-7zc6cbk73lw; Ivor Tossell, "Are These Cats Talking, or Are We Just 'LOL' at Ourselves?" *The Globe and Mail,* May 25, 2007, https://www.theglobeandmail.com/amp/technology/are-these-cats-talking-or-are-we-just-lol-at-ourselves/article1326447/; Erik Hogstrom, "Cat-Tales," *Telegraph Herald* (Dubuque, IA), August 19, 2007; Rutkoff, "With Lolcats Internet Fad"; Bobbie Johnson and Anna Pickard, "How Lolcats Took Over the Web," *The Guardian,* April 28, 2008, https://www.theguardian.com/technology/2008/apr/28/internet.digitalmedia1; Sam Leith, "The Language of Internet Geeks Is No Reason to 'LOL,'" *The Daily Telegraph* (London), March 1, 2008,; "Top 10 Websites for Internet Jokes: U Can Has Humour," *The Daily Telegraph,* September 20,

2008; Sarah Hepola, "The Internet Is Made of Kittens," *Salon*, February 10, 2009, https://www.salon.com/2009/02/10/cat_internet/; Rob Walker, "When Funny Goes Viral," *New York Times Magazine*, July 16, 2010, https://www.nytimes.com/2010/07/18/magazine/18ROFL-t.html?mtrref=undefined&gwh=41281A2B3 2BFF8E84E6BF130924CE23C&gwt=pay&assetType=REGIW ALL; and the inevitable contrarian thinkpiece, Rebecca J. Rosen, "Are Lolcats Making Us Smart?" *The Atlantic*, May 8, 2012, https://www.theatlantic.com/technology/archive/2012/05/are-lolcats-making-us-smart/256830/.

71. Stryker, Epic Win for Anonymous, 80.

72. Kate Miltner, "'There's No Place for Lulz on LOLCats': The Role of Genre, Gender, and Group Identity in the Interpretation and Enjoyment of an Internet Meme," *First Monday*, Volume 19, Number 8 (4 August 2014); https://firstmonday.org/ojs/index.php/fm/article/download/5391/41032014. See also Kate Miltner, "SRSLY Phenomenal: An Investigation into the Appeal of Lolcats" (master's thesis, London School of Economics, 2011).

73. Ibid.

74. Ibid.

75. Miltner, "SRSLY Phenomenal," 33.

76. Luann Daniels, "Internet Cats Are a Hoot and a Half," Something Awful (forum), December 8, 2008, https://www.somethingawful.com/news/luann-cyberdesk-lolcats/1/.

77. Miltner describes the pursuit of mastery (for instance, mastery of the Lolcat dialect, or mastery of the precise timbre of a viral joke) as a major motivation driving the activity of people who spend a great deal of time in internet meme communities (Miltner, "SRSLY Phenomenal").

78. The term *participatory culture*, now a common phrase in media studies, is from Henry Jenkins, *Fans, Bloggers, and Gamers: Exploring Participatory Culture* (New York: New York Uni-

versity Press, 2006). Miltner discusses nostalgia as an element of meme culture in "SRSLY Phenomenal."

79. Adam Downer, "Oh Lawd He Comin'," Know Your Meme (2019).

80. Ryan Milner, The World Made Meme: Public Conversations and Participatory Media (Cambridge, MA: MIT Press, 2016), 8–9.

81. Alissa (@Bantigve), "i can feel he comin in the air tonight / oh lawd." Twitter, January 9, 2019, 8.08 a.m., https://twitter.com/bantigve/status/1083032670852927490?lang=en.

82. Assassin Monkey, "Oh Lawd . . . ," DeviantArt, March 1, 2019, https://www.deviantart.com/assasinmonkey/art/Oh-Lawd-787699680?fbclid=IwAR1v2J1FFeZb8YUeRN8WAjdCb3-5z4sdlYMgJdV8px_HgziHP3f686a75BA.

83. Nicholas Lemann, "Fear Factor," New Yorker, March 27, 2006, https://www.newyorker.com/magazine/2006/03/27/fear-factor.

84. Sara Kiesler, "The Hidden Messages in Computer Networks," Harvard Business Review, January 1986, https://hbr.org/1986/01/the-hidden-messages-in-computer-networks

85. Milner, The World Made Meme, 3.

86. Alejandra Reyes-Velarde, "Aquarium Apologizes after Viral Tweet about 'Thicc' Sea Otter Spawns Harsh Backlash," Los Angeles Times, December 20, 2018, https://www.latimes.com/local/lanow/la-me-ln-sea-otter-backlash-20181220-story.html.

87. Massanari, Participatory Culture, Community, and Play, 1–2.

88. Dong Nguyen, Barbara McGillivray, and Taha Yasseri, "Emo, Love, and God: Making Sense of Urban Dictionary, a Crowd-Sourced Online Dictionary," Royal Society Open Science, May 2, 2018, https://royalsocietypublishing.org/doi/10.1098/rsos.172320; also see the brief but sharp critique of Natalie Rojas (@natalieoffline), Twitter, May 3, 2018.

89. Jean Burgess and Joshua Green, *YouTube* (Cambridge, UK: Polity Press, 2009), 8–9.

90. Melissa Harris-Lacewell, *Barbershops, Bibles, and BET: Everyday Talk and Black Political Thought* (Princeton, NJ: Princeton University Press, 2004), 204.

91. Brad Esposito, "People Are Angry with this Dog-Rating Twitter Account for Changing the Names of Dogs," *BuzzFeed*, June 26, 2018, https://www.buzzfeed.com/bradesposito/people -are-angry-with-this-dog-rating-twitter-account-for.

92. Nicole Hensley, "Donald Trump Briefly Follows Emergency Kittens on Twitter," *New York Daily News*, January 2, 2017, https://www.nydailynews.com/news/politics/donald -trump-briefly-emergency-kittens-twitter-article-1.2931149.

93. Alvin Kernan offers a shrewd analysis of the meaning of canon formation in *Samuel Johnson and the Impact of Print* (Princeton, NJ: Princeton University Press, 1984), especially 241–82.

94. Stryker, *Epic Win for Anonymous,* 86–87.

95. "Nyan Cat in Lobby 7," The MIT Gallery of Hacks, September 6, 2011, http://hacks.mit.edu/Hacks/by_year/2011/ nyan_cat/.

96. See, for example, Alvin Kernan, *Samuel Johnson and the Impact of Print*, and Alvin Kernan, *The Imaginary Library: An Essay on Literature and Society* (Princeton, NJ: Princeton University Press, 1982).

97. Jonathan Zittrain, *The Future of the Internet and How to Stop It* (New Haven, CT: Yale University Press, 2008), 3.

98. Burgess and Green, *YouTube*, 5. See also Jean Burgess, "The iPhone Moment, the Apple Brand, and the Creative Consumer: From 'Hackability and Usability' to Cultural Generativity," in *Studying Mobile Media: Cultural Technologies, Mobile Communication, and the iPhone*, eds. Larissa Hjorth, Jean Burgess, and Ingrid Richardson (New York: Routledge Press, 2012), 28–42.

99. Clay Shirky, Cognitive Surplus: Creativity and Generosity in a Connected Age (New York: Penguin, 2011), 42.

100. Olia Lialina and Dragan Espenschied, eds., *Digital Folklore* (Stuttgart: Merz & Solitude, 2009).

CHAPTER 4

1. See, for example, Ian Hacking, *Historical Ontology* (Cambridge, MA: Harvard University Press, 2004).

2. Writing in 2004, the writer Paul Ford called attention to this beige background, which he first took note of, he says, in a 2004 video called "Numa Numa," which shows a man lip-synching in front of his webcam. Ford argues that the room reflects the empty, standardized character of modern American life, where homes are expensive but drab, manufactured to standard for the sake of efficiency. I suspect that this trope in webcam videos from the 2000s also reflects fears about the unknown audience of these videos. Paul Ford, "The American Room," *The Message* (blog), Medium, July 30, 2004, https://medium.com/message/the-american-room-3fce9b2b98c5.

3. Dave Barry, *Dave Barry in Cyberspace* (New York: Crown, 1996), 159. I remember reading this book in 1996; I found the description of the Coffee Cam useful because my home didn't have fast enough internet speeds for me to experience the site on my family's computer. The Trojan Room Coffee Cam ended its run in 2001.

4. From the site's FAQ: "In addition to the cat, you are often seeing our carpet, a purple and grey mottled industrial variety, our conference room chairs, black lacquered wood with blue-striped seats, and the underside of our conference room table, black wood top with metal legs. Between Noon and 1330, US Pacific Time (GMT-8), you're seeing the legs and feet of JointSolutions staff members eating lunch at the table.

Depending on camera angle, you're occasionally seeing staff thighs, too. This is a feature, not a bug." "KittyCam Frequently Asked Questions," KittyCam, Web Archive, December 2, 1998, https://web.archive.org/web/19990218104454/http:/www.kittycam.com:80/html/faq.html.

5. Ibid., Web Archive, February 8, 1998; Eppink, "How Cats Took over the Internet."

6. George Mannes, "Don't Give Up on The Web," CNN Money, February 1, 2001, https://money.cnn.com/magazines/fsb/fsb_archive/2001/02/01/296267/index.htm.

7. "KittyCam Frequently Asked Questions," December 2, 1998.

8. Eppink, "How Cats Took over the Internet." Exhibition at the Museum of the Moving Image, New York City, 2015. See, for example, "Mr. Pugsly," Pet of the Day, December 11, 1997, https://web.archive.org/web/19971211155254/http://www.petoftheday.com:80/.

9. Eppink, "How Cats Took over the Internet." See, for example, "Puskin," Cat of the Day, May 11, 2000, https://web.archive.org/web/20000511104045/http://www.catoftheday.com:80/.

10. "Cat Scan Contest," June 19, 2000, https://web.archive.org/web/20000619211159/http://www.cat-scan.com:80/Old/entries.html.

11. Megan Doscher, "A Web Contest Proves There Is More Than One Way to Scan a Cat," *Wall Street Journal*, August 7, 1998.

12. Bleszinski reported receiving angry letters and referrals to animal cruelty organizations. He also said that the cats were in no danger and that he disqualified any picture in which a cat seemed to be in pain (Ibid.). Then again, he noted with pleasure that his site received recognition as the Cruel Site of the Day, one of the unofficial "awards" that used to go around in

the early days of the web. "Press Awards this stoopid Site Has Earned," Cat Scan Contest, Web Archive, June 2000, https://web.archive.org/web/20000620224313/http:/www.cat-scan.com:80/Old/press.html.

13. "Bonsai Kitten," Internet Archive, February 2, 2001, https://web.archive.org/web/20010202065200/http://bonsaikitten.com/.

14. I remember sitting against the lockers one day in high school and listening to a friend describe the site. I don't remember whether she said it was a hoax. We had no way of viewing the site together unless one visited the other's house to look at the family computer.

15. Eppink, "How Cats Took over the Internet." In case you're wondering which law the site broke, it was possibly "a 1999 federal statute that makes it a federal felony to possess 'a depiction of animal cruelty' with the intent to distribute across state lines—such as on the Internet." Bill Hoffman, "Furor over 'Bonsai Kitten' Site," *New York Post*, February 12, 2001, https://nypost.com/2001/02/12/furor-over-bonsai-kitten-site/. MIT complied with the subpoena; it also took the site off their server.

16. Eppink, "How Cats Took over the Internet." "Bonsai Kitten," The Museum of Hoaxes, accessed August 6, 2018, http://hoaxes.org/archive/permalink/bonsai_kitten.

17. Justine Hankins, "Tangled Web of Cruelty," *The Guardian*, April 12, 2003, https://www.theguardian.com/uk/2003/apr/12/animalwelfare.world.

18. Eppink, "How Cats Took over the Internet"; Jim Edgar, "About," My Cat Hates You, January 1, 2016, http://www.mycathatesyou.com/about-us/.

19. James Edgar, *My Cat Hates You* (London: Hodder & Stoughton, 2004); James Edgar, *Bad Cat: 244 Not-So-Pretty Kittens and Cats Gone Bad* (New York: Workman Publishing, 2004).

20. Quotation and website citations from Eppink, "How Cats Took over the Internet."

21. Eppink, "How Cats Took over the Internet"; "The Infinite Cats Project," Internet Archive, June 11, 2004, https://web .archive.org/web/20040611012221/; http://www.infinitecat.com: 80/infinite/cat1.html.

22. Randy Malamud, *An Introduction to Animals and Visual Culture* (New York: Palgrave Macmillan, 2012), 37.

23. "No Digital Camera?" The Infinite Cat Project, Internet Archive, December 30, 2005, https://web.archive.org/web/ 20051230034623/www.infinitecat.com/.

The other aspect of the past that the Infinite Cat Project reconjures is the sense of isolation that once attended internet use. Today, the internet is all around us: on phone screens, on watch faces, in home assistant devices like Alexa, in portable laptops. Within a single generation's memory, however, people encountered the internet mostly while sitting alone in front of desktop computers. In that sense, the gallery preserves the soul of an earlier internet, when to be online was to be *alone together*, in Sherry Turkle's term, without any illusions about it. Sherry Turkle, *Alone Together: Why We Expect More from Technology and Less from Each Other* (New York: Basic Books, 2011).

24. Eppink, "How Cats Took over the Internet"; Wired staff, "Cat Gets Hit(s)," *Wired*, February 23, 2002; "Cat Is Net Celebrity," *Birmingham Post*, January 16, 2003.

25. David Sapsted, "4m See Cat's Recovery on the Net," *The Daily Telegraph*, January 16, 2003.

26. David Donnan, quoted in Lucy Mcdonald, "A Game of Cat and Mouse for Frank the Online Feline," *Mail on Sunday*, May 17, 2002.

27. Ibid.

28. Eppink, "How Cats Took over the Internet"; Sarah Boxer, "Internet's Best Friend (Let Me Count the Ways)," *New*

York Times, July 30, 2005, https://www.nytimes.com/2005/
07/30/arts/internets-best-friend-let-me-count-the-ways.html.
The argument that we chose cats as the mascot of the internet
because they remind us of the voyeuristic pleasures of the internet was very much in keeping with the themes of discourse
about the internet in the mid-2000s. The blogger Emily Gould
wrote when she started work as an editor at Gawker in 2006,
the site's previous editor, Jessica Coen, told her "that the commenters loved it when she revealed personal details. Not only
did I find this to be true, I found it to be almost necessary."
Emily Gould, "Exposed," *New York Times Magazine*, May 25,
2008, https://www.nytimes.com/2008/05/25/magazine/25internet-t
.html. In 2008, *Webster's New World Dictionary* selected *over-
share* as its word of the year.

29. Mary Savig, curator of manuscripts at the Archives of
American Art, in discussion with the author, May 15, 2017. The
exhibition was titled *Before Internet Cats: Feline Finds from the
Archives of American Art* (April 28–October 29, 2017). Savig
reported that cats and dogs appeared in roughly equal proportions in the archives she consulted.

30. 4chan reportedly began its "Caturday" tradition in early
2005, a few months before the *Times* piece came out. In a blog post
on *Time Magazine*'s TechLand, writer Lev Grossman published an
email from one of his readers that dated Caturday to early 2005:
"There is more than enough EXIF data scattered around the internet to prove that cat macros are ancient, by internet standards.
Caturday, for example, was a meme on a 4chan.org imageboard
which originated around the beginning of 2005 as a protest against
\"Furry Friday\" threads (in which basement-dwelling creeps
would post anthropomorphic disney characters giving [sorry, gotta
go family values at this point].") Lev Grossman, "Lolcats Adden-
dum: Where I Got the Story Wrong," *Techland* (blog), *Time*, July
16, 2007, http://techland.time.com/2007/07/16/.

31. Jamie Dubs, "Advice Dog." *Know Your Meme*, accessed August 7, 2018, https://knowyourmeme.com/memes/advice -dog.

32. Nicholas Carr, *The Big Switch: Rewiring the World from Edison to Google* (New York: W.W. Norton & Company, 2008), 129–30. The video is called "Pajamas and Nick Drake," and you can still view it on YouTube today.

33. Kevin Alloca, *Videocracy: How YouTube Is Changing the World . . . with Double Rainbows, Singing Foxes, and Other Trends We Can't Stop Watching* (New York: Bloomsbury, 2018), 224. I suspect that he does not have numbers to back up the tacit claim that, by the time "Friday" came out, cat videos were doing extremely well, compared with other kinds of videos. Otherwise he would have shown the numbers. He trusts that the internet-cat connection will resonate with his readers even without supporting data.

34. Stuart Dredge, "YouTube: The Most Popular Cats from Its First Ten Years," *The Guardian*, May 18, 2015, https://www .theguardian.com/technology/2015/may/18/youtube-most -popular-cats-maru-grumpy-cat.

35. Eppink, "How Cats Took over the Internet."

36. Andy Capper and Juliette Eisner, dirs., *Lil Bub & Friendz* (produced by Juliette Eisner, premiered at the Tribeca Film Festival, April 18, 2013).

37. Gideon Lewis-Kraus, "In Search of the Heart of the Online Cat-Industrial Complex," *Wired*, August 31, 2012, https:// www.wired.com/2012/08/ff-cats/.

38. Ibid.

39. Eppink, "How Cats Took over the Internet."

40. Chris Anderson, *The Long Tail: Why the Future of Business Is Selling Less of More* (New York: Hyperion, 2006).

41. However, Anderson's prediction that internet microfame would overtake the old-fashioned blockbuster economy was

premature. See Anita Elberse, *Blockbusters: Hit-Making, Risk-Taking, and the Big Business of Entertainment* (New York: Henry Holt and Company, 2013), 157–58.

42. Elberse, *Blockbusters*, 159. Anderson takes this kind of data into account in an updated edition of his book, titled *The Longer Long Tail: How Endless Choice Is Creating Unlimited Demand* (London: Random House, 2009).

43. Elberse, *Blockbusters*, 159–64. See also Erik Brynjolfsson, Yu (Jeffrey) Hu, and Michael D. Smith, "Tails vs. Superstars: The Effect of Information Technology on Product Variety and Sales Concentration Patterns," *Information Systems Research* 21, no. 4 (December 2010): 736–47.

44. Eppink, "How Cats Took over the Internet"; Rachel Swatman, "Meet Maru 'Mugumogu'—the Cardboard Box–Loving, Record-Breaking Cat," *Guinness World Records* (blog), March 24, 2017, https://www.guinnessworldrecords.com/news/2017/3/video-meet-maru-mugumogu—the cardboard box-loving-record-breaking-cat?fb_comment_id=1266691013414763_1454566414627221.

45. Lewis-Kraus, "In Search of the Heart of the Online Cat-Industrial Complex."

46. Ibid.

47. Ibid.

48. The show is called "Daisuki! Itsutsugo," and you can view the theme song on YouTube (https://www.youtube.com/watch?v=7ALUHGmn5hk).

49. For example, this exchange between Bridavisky and a television reporter in Capper and Eisner, *Lil Bub & Friendz*:

> REPORTER: How did she get so famous? Is it the mouth? Is it the extra toes? What do you think it is about Lil Bub?
>
> BRIDAVISKY: I think it's everything. She's probably the most amazing creature on the planet.

See also Summer Anne Burton, "Meet Lil Bub, Nature's 'Happy Accident' Who Is about to Win Your Heart," *BuzzFeed*, June 30, 2012, https://www.buzzfeed.com/summeranne/meet-lil-bub -natures-happy-accident-who-is.

50. See, for example, Anna Breslaw, "And Then Dwarf Cat Li'l Bub Happened and Everything Changed," *Jezebel*, July 4, 2012, https://jezebel.com/471356420#!.

51. Eppink, "How Cats Took over the Internet." See, for example, Anna Breslaw, "And Then Dwarf Cat Lil' Bub Happened and Everything Changed."

52. Bridavisky has a lot of good quotes in the documentary. Here he is discussing the first time he wore a Lil Bub T-shirt after his friend printed off a set: "I wore them the first day we had them, before Bub was really famous. And there was this little girl eating breakfast across from us, and she looks over at me. And she's like, 'Mommy, mommy, I want that cat.' And that's when I knew that Bub was going to be *fucking famous*." Capper and Eisner, *Lil Bub & Friendz*.

53. Angela Watercutter, "Lil Bub, the Internet's Cutest Cat, Is Building a Not-So-Little Media Empire," *Wired*, September 13, 2013, https://www.wired.com/2013/09/lil-bub/.

54. Capper and Eisner, *Lil Bub & Friendz*.

55. Max Read, "How to Get Rich from Memes: Steal Other Memes," *Gawker*, September 30, 2013, https://gawker.com/how -to-get-rich-on-memes-steal-other-memes-1426797890.

56. "Meet Grumpy Cat," Reddit, accessed December 2, 2019, https://www.reddit.com/r/pics/comments/10bu17/meet_ grumpy_cat/.

57. "I am the owner of Tard the Grumpy Cat, AMAA" Reddit, accessed December 2, 2019, https://www.reddit.com/r/ casualiama/comments/113c69/i_am_the_owner_of_tard_the_ grumpy_cat_amaa/.

58. Eppink, "How Cats Took over the Internet."

59. Laura Northrup, "Grumpy Cat Coffee Drink Only the Newest Piece of Internet-Famous Cat Merchandise," *Consumerist*, July 30, 2013.

60. Eppink, "How Cats Took over the Internet"; *Grumpy Cat's Worst Christmas Ever*, dir. Tim Hill (Lifetime, 2014).

61. This being New York City, I assume they actually said, "No *fuckin'* way."

62. Capper and Eisner, *Lil Bub & Friendz*.

63. Matt Taghioff, in discussion with the author, August 3, 2018.

64. Curious Zelda (@CuriousZelda), "RUN FOR YOUR LIVES," October 18, 2017, 4:03 a.m., https://twitter.com/Curious Zelda/status/920606204795277314; Curious Zelda (@Curious Zelda), "Suddenly," May 11, 2018, 1:12 p.m., https://twitter.com/CuriousZelda/status/995034034697883649.

65. Curious Zelda (@CuriousZelda), "There's no such thing," February 18, 2017, 4:30 a.m., https://twitter.com/CuriousZelda/status/832930400636960768; Curious Zelda (@CuriousZelda), "Today," September 26, 2017, 4:53 a.m., https://twitter.com/CuriousZelda/status/912646204974096384.

66. Curious Zelda (@CuriousZelda), "Always leave your Zelda in the folded position," November 29, 2017, 12:35 p.m., https://twitter.com/CuriousZelda/status/935970579508842497; Curious Zelda (@CuriousZelda), "Please be careful," October 22, 2017, 12:21 p.m., https://twitter.com/CuriousZelda/status/922181019264061441.

67. Curious Zelda (@CuriousZelda), "See a house fly," June 20, 2018, 11:24 a.m., https://twitter.com/CuriousZelda/status/1009502381703421954.

68. Curious Zelda (@CuriousZelda), "I thought I saw my nemesis," June 4, 2018, 12:13 p.m., https://twitter.com/Curious Zelda/status/1003716459711918081.

69. Curious Zelda (@CuriousZelda), "Scratch the sofa," September 11, 2017, 9:12 a.m., https://twitter.com/CuriousZelda/status/907275752835567617.

70. Floor (@Krentebal), "Can't get enough of @Curious Zelda," January 21, 2018, 11:46 a.m., https://twitter.com/Krentebal/status/955164608280526848; Spoony Holidays (@spoonfayse), "seems I'm doodling tuxedo cats," September 19, 2017, 4:13 p.m., https://twitter.com/spoonfayse/status/910280773240070146; Mogon (@mogonv), "It was @CuriousZelda's birthday last week," February 8, 2018, 10:07 a.m., https://twitter.com/mogonv/status/961662753789259776; One Fine Weasel (@onefineweasel), "Fifty one years old and still doing fan art," February 27, 2018, 1:37 p.m., https://twitter.com/onefineweasel/status/968601023643 299840; Glusix (@Glusix), "Just because," March 18, 2018, 11:14 a.m., https://twitter.com/Glusix_/status/975435215857504256; Monica (@Monica_ion), "Warmups this morning," March 22, 2018, 3:36 a.m., https://twitter.com/Monica_ion/status/976769574237605 888; https://twitter.com/its_Shenanigan/status/98226772732157 9520; m. a. tateishi (@matateishi), "Tiny paintings inspired by @ CuriousZelda," April 18, 2018, 5:03 a.m., https://twitter.com/matateishi/status/986575834721828864; https://twitter.com/brocoarts/status/987151927808086016; Famos Zwiebel-Heinrich (@meckermieze), April 21, 2018, 3:20 p.m., https://twitter.com/NomNomNom_x3/status/987818398410297345; SlamDunkFish (@FishDunk), "@CuriousZelda it was fun to paint Zelda!" April 24, 2018, 8:31 a.m., https://twitter.com/FishDunk/status/98880263417 6958464; Rock n Roll Queen (@Strillersthecat), "A little doodle of @CuriousZelda today," May 10, 2018, 9:48 a.m., https://twitter.com/strillersthecat/status/994620311558606848; Cristal Math (@ Zoey Cocamotes), "@Curious Zelda a wee drawering for ye," May 19, 2018, 6:06 p.m., https://twitter.com/ZoeyCocamotes/status/998006966319566848; Claire Ingram (@claireingramart), "I love @CuriousZelda's little face!" June 3, 2018, 12:06 p.m., https://

twitter.com/claireingramart/status/1003352290110201856; Mari-
anne Martin (@MariMartinis), "@CuriousZelda The face of love,"
June 19, 2018, 7:57 a.m., https://twitter.com/MariMartinis/status/
1009087907007787008; Chelsea Kuran (@Chelseakuran), "This
is @CuriousZelda," August 6, 2018, 10:12 a.m., https://twitter.
com/chelseakuran/status/1026516360019369985.

71. He didn't tell me about this; I read it firsthand on Twitter. Source anonymous to protect the thirsty.

72. Franco Moretti, "The Slaughterhouse of Literature,"
Modern Language Quarterly 61, no. 1 (2000): 207–209.

73. Arthur De Vany and W. David Walls, "Bose-Einstein
Dynamics and Adaptive Contracting in the Motion Picture
Industry," *Economic Journal* 106, no. 439 (November 1996):
1493–1505.

74. Moretti, "The Slaughterhouse of Literature," 207–13.

75. Lewis-Kraus, "In Search of the Heart of the Online Cat-
Industrial Complex."